Lecture Notes in Computer Science 4920

Commenced Publication in 1973
Founding and Former Series Editors:
Gerhard Goos, Juris Hartmanis, and Jan van Leeuwen

Yun Q. Shi (Ed.)

Transactions on Data Hiding and Multimedia Security III

 Springer

Volume Editor

Yun Q. Shi
New Jersey Institute of Technology
Newark, NJ, 07102, USA
E-mail: shi@njit.edu

Library of Congress Control Number: 2008927739

CR Subject Classification (1998): K.4.1, K.6.5, H.5.1, D.4.6, E.3, E.4, F.2.2, H.3, I.4

LNCS Sublibrary: SL 4 – Security and Cryptology

ISSN   1861-3043
ISBN-10   3-540-69016-6 Springer Berlin Heidelberg New York
ISBN-13   978-3-540-69016-0 Springer Berlin Heidelberg New York

Springer is a part of Springer Science+Business Media

springer.com

© Springer-Verlag Berlin Heidelberg 2008

Typesetting: Camera-ready by author, data conversion by Scientific Publishing Services, Chennai, India
Printed on acid-free paper   SPIN: 12280889   06/3180   5 4 3 2 1 0

Preface

In this volume, we present the third issue of the *LNCS Transactions on Data Hiding and Multimedia Security*. Continuing the tradition of the previous two editions, we are delighted to present contributions in the areas of steganography and digital watermarking.

The first two papers in this issue deal with the security of steganographic systems. It is already widely accepted that the application of covering codes to data embedding can improve both the embedding efficiency and the security of steganographic schemes. In the first paper, Bierbrauer and Fridrich describe several families of covering codes, allowing a better performance compared to linear codes which are currently in use in steganography. In the second paper, Korzhik et al. propose to customize the notion of the Bhattacharyya distance in order to measure the detectability of steganographic systems through steganalysis. In the third paper, Jamzad and Kermani present a novel image steganographic scheme based on Gabor filters and neural networks.

Finally, this volume contains two papers dealing with digital watermarking and data hiding. In the fourth paper, Venturini introduces and analyzes a new covert channel, called the timing channel, and proposes countermeasures to reduce its capacity. Finally, in the fifth paper, Vila-Forcén et al. analyze the performance of additive attacks against quantization-based data-hiding methods.

We hope that this issue is of great interest to the data-hiding community and that these papers will trigger new research in the field of data hiding and multimedia security.

Finally, we want to thank all the authors, reviewers and editors who have devoted their valuable time to the success of this third issue. As always, special thanks go to Springer and Alfred Hofmann for their continuous support.

January 2008

Yun Q. Shi (Editor-in-Chief)
Hyoung-Joong Kim (Vice Editor-in-Chief)
Stefan Katzenbeisser (Vice Editor-in-Chief)

LNCS Transactions on
Data Hiding and Multimedia Security

Editorial Board

Advisory Board

Table of Contents

Constructing Good Covering Codes for Applications in
Steganography.. 1
Jürgen Bierbrauer and Jessica Fridrich

On the Use of Bhattacharyya Distance as a Measure of the Detectability
of Steganographic Systems 23
Valery Korzhik, Hideki Imai, Junji Shikata,
Guillermo Morales-Luna, and Ekaterina Gerling

Secure Steganography Using Gabor Filter and Neural Networks 33
Mansour Jamzad and Zahra Zahedi Kermani

Oracle Channels 50
Ilaria Venturini

Quantization-Based Methods: Additive Attacks Performance
Analysis 70
J.E. Vila-Forcén, S. Voloshynovskiy, O. Koval,
F. Pérez-González, and T. Pun

Author Index 91

Constructing Good Covering Codes for Applications in Steganography

Jürgen Bierbrauer[1] and Jessica Fridrich[2]

[1] Department of Mathematical Sciences
Michigan Technological University
HOUGHTON (MI) 49931, USA
[2] Department of Electrical and Computer Engineering
Binghamton University
BINGHAMTON (NY) 13902-6000

Abstract. Application of covering codes to data embedding improves embedding efficiency and security of steganographic schemes. In this paper, we describe several familes of covering codes constructed using the blockwise direct sum of factorizations. We show that non-linear constructions offer better performance compared to simple linear covering codes currently used by steganographers. Implementation details are given for a selected code family.

1 Introduction

Steganography is the art of stealth communication. Its purpose is to make communication undetectable. The steganography problem is also known as the prisoners' dilemma formulated by Simmons [28]. Alice and Bob are imprisoned and want to hatch an escape plan. They are allowed to communicate via a channel monitored by a warden. If the warden finds out that they are communicating secretly, he throws them into solitary confinement. Thus, the prisoners need to design a method to exchange messages without raising the warden's suspicion.

The prisoners hide their messages in innocuous-looking cover objects by slightly modifying them (obtaining stego objects). The embedding process is usually driven by a stego key, which is a secret shared between Alice and Bob. It is typically used to select a subset of the cover object and the order in which the cover object elements are visited during embedding.

The most important property of any steganographic communication is statistical undetectability. In other words, the warden should not be able to distinguish between cover and stego objects. Formal description of this requirement in information-theoretic terms was given by Cachin [4]. If the communication channel that Alice and Bob use is distortion-free, we speak about the passive warden scenario.

Digital multimedia files, such as digital images, audio, or video, are conveniently used in steganography today because they are digitized forms of physical quantities, such as photon counts or voltages, and thus contain certain small level

Y.Q. Shi (Ed.): Transactions on DHMS III, LNCS 4920, pp. 1–22, 2008.

of noise. Because of the presence of this indeterministic component, steganographers hope that part of this component can be replaced with pseudo-random (e.g., encrypted) message bits, thus obtaining a secure steganographic method.

Intuitively, the fewer changes the embedding process incurs, the smaller the chance that the embedding modifications will be statistically detectable. We acknowledge, though, that the number of changes is not the only important factor influencing the security of the steganographic scheme. The choice of the cover object and the character of modifications play an equally important role. For example, it is known that embedding in spatial domain of a decompressed JPEG image can be easily detectable even when only one embedding change is carried out [15]. Furthermore, the impact of embedding realized by flipping LSBs of pixels (Least Significant Bit) is relatively easy to detect even at very low embedding rates [22]. Nevertheless, it is true that for two steganographic schemes with the same embedding mechanism, the one that introduces fewer embedding changes will be more secure.

Steganographers use the concept of embedding efficiency to quantify how effectively a given algorithm embeds data. The embedding efficiency is defined [32] as the average number of random message bits embedded using one embedding change. There is evidence that schemes with low embedding efficiency offer worse security than schemes with higher efficiency. For example, the popular JPEG steganography program OutGuess [26] embeds messages in DCT coefficients (Discrete Cosine Transform) in two passes. In the first pass, it embeds with efficiency 2 by matching the LSBs of DCT coefficients with message bits. In the second pass, more changes are imposed on the previously non-visited DCT coefficients. While this has the benefit of preserving the global DCT histogram, the embedding efficiency decreases significantly. On the other hand, the Model based Steganography (MBS) [27] without deblocking preserves even more statistics than OutGuess and does so at a higher embedding efficiency. Steganalysis of both schemes [14] indicates that MBS is significantly harder to detect than OutGuess.

The importance of high embedding efficiency for steganography and the relevance of covering codes to this problem were recognized for the first time by Crandall [7], who showed that linear codes can markedly improve the embedding efficiency. He called this type of embedding "matrix embedding", which was made popular in the stego community by Westfeld in his F5 algorithm [32].

Crandall refers to an unpublished article by Bierbrauer [2] that provides deeper insight into this problem from the point of view of a coding theorist. The connection between linear covering codes and steganography has also appeared in the paper by Galand and Kabatiansky [17] who addressed both the passive and active warden scenarios.

In this paper, we describe and extend the original Bierbrauer's work. We believe that the steganographic community will benefit from this work as it formulates the problem of embedding efficiency in coding-theoretic language and makes a connection with a large body of work in coding. Moreover, we point out the importance of certain families of codes to steganography and show that non-linear codes have better performance than known linear constructions, e.g., matrix embedding.

In Section 2, the connection between covering functions and steganography is formally established. In Sections 3, we show how coding-theoretic bounds translate to bounds on basic descriptors of steganographic schemes. Section 4 contains basic methods for constructing good covering codes (good in the sense of providing high steganographic embedding efficiency). In Section 5, we study some good families of non-linear codes. Section 6 lists the best currently known covering functions that we expect to find applications in steganography. The embedding efficiency of steganographic schemes that use these covering functions is compared and contrasted to theoretical bounds in Section 7. To enable practical implementation of steganographic schemes that use the proposed constructions, in Section 8 we describe the details of the non-linear Nordstrom-Robinson code and some covering functions related to it. While the description is more involved than in the linear case, the resulting algorithm is very efficient. The paper is concluded in Section 9.

2   The Link to Coding Theory

For concreteness, we assume that the cover object used for communication is a grayscale digital image whose pixels are integers between 0 and 255. We assign a bit to each pixel value (the LSB of the grayscale value). We will further assume that the embedding mechanism is flipping the LSB, while stressing that other embedding operations or bit assignments are certainly possible. We also assume that the sender can use all pixels for embedding, i.e., the embedding is not constrained to any selection channel [13]. Possible directions one can take for application of covering codes to non-trivial selection channels (wet paper codes) were briefly discussed in [13].

Let us assume that the embedding proceeds by blocks. The cover image is divided into disjoint segments of N pixels. Let $x = (x_1, x_2, \ldots, x_N)$ be the bitstring formed by their least significant bits. Here we view the entries, the bits, as elements of the field $\mathbb{F}_2 = \{0, 1\}$. Formally we can write $x \in \mathbb{F}_2^N$. Assume the secret message has been encoded as a bitstring. We scan this bitstring and divide it into segments of length n, for some number $n < N$. What we want to construct is a suitable function f, which maps bitstrings of length N to bitstrings of length n, formally

$$f : \mathbb{F}_2^N \longrightarrow \mathbb{F}_2^n,$$

which allows us to extract n bits of the secret message. This means that for given $x \in \mathbb{F}_2^N$ (the LSBs of the corresponding segment of the cover image) and $y \in \mathbb{F}_2^n$ (a segment of the secret message) we want to replace x by x' such that $f(x') = y$. An important question is the relation between x and x'. If x and x' differ in 3 of their N coordinates, then that means that 3 of our segment of N pixels need to be changed. Our goal is to keep that number of changes to a minimum. The number of coordinates where the entries of two strings x, x' differ is a basic notion of coding theory. It is the **Hamming distance** $d(x, x')$. If we want to control the worst case, then we fix an upper bound ρ on the embedding distortion $d(x, x')$. This leads to the following notion:

Definition 1. *A **covering function** $COV(\rho, N, n)$ is a mapping*

$$f : \mathbb{F}_2^N \longrightarrow \mathbb{F}_2^n$$

which satisfies the following: for every $x \in \mathbb{F}_2^N$, $y \in \mathbb{F}_2^n$ there is some $x' \in \mathbb{F}_2^N$ such that $d(x, x') \leq \rho$ and $f(x') = y$.

A covering function $COV(\rho, N, n)$ enables construction of a steganographic scheme that can embed n bits in N pixels using *at most* ρ embedding changes. We say that the scheme has **relative capacity** $\alpha = n/N$, **change rate** ρ/N, and **embedding efficiency** $e = \alpha/(\rho/N) = n/\rho$. We remark here that the embedding efficiency in steganography is typically defined in a slightly different manner as the *expected* number of bits embedded per one embedding change, where the expectation is taken over all possible covers $x \in \mathbb{F}_2^N$ and messages. More on this difference is included in Section 7.

We now switch to terminology more commonly used in coding. For readers not familiar with coding theory, we recommend the introductory text [1]. Calling N the **length,** n the **redundancy**, and ρ the **covering radius**, the following design problems arise:

- We want n/N, the **relative redundancy**, to be large
  (large relative capacity).
- We want ρ/N, the **relative covering radius**, to be small to have good embedding efficiency.
- Finally, there should be an effective algorithm that calculates x'.

In coding theory, a **code** is defined simply as a subset of the space of all tuples of a certain length N over some alphabet, where N is the length of the code. We speak of a binary code if the alphabet has two elements. Historically, coding theory developed in the context of information transmission over noisy channels. Typically in these applications the most important parameter is the **minimum distance** d : any two different elements of the code should be at Hamming distance $\geq d$. In other words, if two elements of the code (**codewords**) are different, then they are very different. In our context, the basic parameter is the covering radius:

Definition 2. *Let $\mathcal{C} \subset \mathbb{F}_2^N$. The **covering radius** of the code $\mathcal{C}$ is the smallest number ρ such that any N-tuple is at Hamming distance $\leq \rho$ from some codeword.*

Informally, one speaks of error-correcting codes if the minimum distance is the important parameter, of covering codes if one is more interested in the covering radius. While the minimum distance concerns only the distances between codewords (in a way it ignores the ambient space $\mathbb{F}_2^N$), the covering radius is defined in terms of the embedding of the code in its ambient space.

Definition 1 demands that the inverse image $f^{-1}(y)$ be a covering code of radius ρ for every choice of $y \in \mathbb{F}_2^n$. It follows that $\mathbb{F}_2^N$ is the disjoint union of 2^n such covering codes. Clearly, this is an equivalent description of a covering function:

Theorem 1. *The following are equivalent:*

- *A covering function $COV(\rho, N, n)$.*
- *A partition of $\mathbb{F}_2^N$ into 2^n covering codes of covering radius ρ.*

We now give an example of a covering function constructed from a linear code. This was also discussed, for example, in [32]. Start from the matrix

$$H = \begin{pmatrix} 1\,0\,0\,1\,1\,0\,1 \\ 0\,1\,0\,1\,0\,1\,1 \\ 0\,0\,1\,0\,1\,1\,1 \end{pmatrix}$$

whose entries are elements of $\mathbb{F}_2$. Consider the linear mapping $f : \mathbb{F}_2^7 \longrightarrow \mathbb{F}_2^3$ defined by $f(x_1, x_2, x_3, x_4, x_5, x_6, x_7) = (y_1, y_2, y_3)$, where

$$y_1 = x_1 + x_4 + x_5 + x_7, \ y_2 = x_2 + x_4 + x_6 + x_7, \ y_3 = x_3 + x_5 + x_6 + x_7.$$

This function can be described in terms of matrix H. In fact, y_i is the dot product of x and the i-th row of H. We claim that f is a $COV(1, 7, 3)$.

For example, $f(0011010) = 100$. Assume $y = 111$. We claim that it is possible to replace $x = 0011010$ by x' such that $f(x') = 111$ and $d(x, x') = 1$. In fact, we claim more: the coordinate where x has to be changed is uniquely determined. In our case, this is coordinate number 6, so $x' = 0011000$. Here is the general embedding rule: form $f(x) + y$ (in the example this is 011). Find the column of H which has these entries (in our example, this is the sixth column). This marks the coordinate where x needs to be changed to embed payload y. This procedure indicates how H and f were constructed and how this can be generalized: the columns of H are simply all nonzero 3-tuples in some order.

In general, we start from our choice of n and write a matrix H whose columns consist of all nonzero n-tuples. Then H has $N = 2^n - 1$ columns. The covering function $f : \mathbb{F}_2^N \longrightarrow \mathbb{F}_2^n$ is defined by way of the dot products with the rows of H, just as in the example $n = 3$. Then f is a covering function of radius 1 giving us the following theorem.

Theorem 2. *For every n there is a $COV(1, 2^n - 1, n)$.*

These covering functions are well-known not only in coding theory but also in the steganographic community [32]. They are equivalent to the binary **Hamming codes** and are by definition **linear** (over $\mathbb{F}_2$). Every linear covering function can of course be described in terms of an (n, N)-matrix H. Obviously the covering radius will be $\leq \rho$ if and only if every vector from $\mathbb{F}_2^n$ can be written as a linear combination of at most ρ columns of H. As 0-columns and repeated columns are not helpful for this purpose, we may as well assume that the columns of H are distinct and nonzero. The code $f^{-1}(0)$ is a linear covering code of radius ρ. Vice versa, it is also clear that the existence of such a covering code can be used to construct H and f. The matrix H is known as a **check matrix** of the code. We have just proved the following theorem:

Theorem 3. *The following are equivalent:*

- *A linear $COV(\rho, N, n)$.*
- *A binary linear code of length N and dimension $N - n$ of covering radius ρ.*
- *A collection of N nonzero bitstrings of length n with the property that every element of $\mathbb{F}_2^n$ can be written as a sum of at most ρ bitstrings from the collection.*

The description of covering functions in terms of covering codes was first given by Crandall [7] who references [2]. The textbook [1] contains a description, which is more general in that it considers arbitrary alphabets. Here we concentrate on the binary case as it is by far the most interesting. Galand and Kabatiansky [17] treat the case of the description corresponding to linear covering codes. In Section 4, we are going to see that non-linear constructions can in fact be very powerful.

For readers who are interested in more technical material on covering codes and wider connections to other mathematical disciplines, we now include a brief discussion supplied with appropriate references.

The notion of covering functions was introduced in [2,1] in a slightly more general form, using arbitrary alphabets. Definition 1 is the binary case. Covering codes are classical objects in coding theory. A recent book on the subject is *Covering codes* by Cohen, Honkala, Litsyn and Lobstein [6]. By Theorem 1 a covering function is equivalent with a partition of the ambient space into covering codes. These partitions have been studied by the coding community. In Etzion-Greenberg [11], they appear under the name *covering by coverings*.

There is also a graph-theoretic link. In fact, the graph-theoretic problem is more general. It applies to any graph G. The problem we are interested in arises as the special case when G is a Hamming graph (the vertices are the bitstrings of length N, two bitstrings form an edge if their distance is 1). A ρ-**dominating** set D of graph G is defined as a set of vertices, such that each vertex of G has distance $\leq \rho$ from a vertex of D. The ρ-**domatic number** of graph G is the smallest number of subsets when the vertices are partitioned into ρ-dominating sets. This notion seems to go back to Zelinka [33] and Carnielli [5]. More information on the subject is in Östergård [24].

3   Coding-Theoretic Bounds and Linear Constructions

As explained in the introduction, to minimize the statistical impact of embedding, the steganographic scheme should have high embedding efficiency. In terms of covering functions $COV(\rho, N, n)$, we would like to know for what values of the three parameters covering functions exist and which functions allow high embedding efficiency n/ρ. In this section, we first establish a useful inequality that will give us bounds on the maximal achievable embedding efficiency. Then, we give examples of linear covering functions that can be used in steganography directly or as ingredients in more advanced constructions described in Section 5. We start with some simple recursive constructions.

Proposition 1. *If $COV(\rho_i, N_i, n_i)$ exist for $i = 1, 2, \ldots$, then $COV(\sum \rho_i, \sum N_i, \sum n_i)$ exists.*

The existence of $COV(\rho, N, n)$ implies the existence of

$$COV(\rho + 1, N, n), \ COV(\rho, N + 1, n), \ COV(\rho, N, n - 1)$$

and of $COV(c \cdot \rho, c \cdot N, c \cdot n)$ for every natural number c.

This hardly needs a proof. For the first property simply write your bitstring of length $\sum N_i$ as a concatenation of strings of length N_i each and apply the $COV(\rho_i, N_i, n_i)$ to the corresponding segment. The rest is equally obvious and follows immediately from the definition. For example, using the stego terminology, if we can embed n bits using at most ρ changes in N pixels, it is certainly true that we can embed the same payload in the same pixels using at most $\rho + 1$ changes, etc.

In order to obtain a bound connecting the three parameters of a covering function, observe that the existence of a $COV(\rho, N, n)$ implies the existence of a covering code with at most 2^{N-n} codewords. This is because the sets $f^{-1}(y), y \in \mathbb{F}_2^n$ partition the ambient space $\mathbb{F}_2^N$. Each codeword thus determines $\sum_{i=0}^{\rho} \binom{N}{i}$ vectors at Hamming distance at most ρ. Adding up all those numbers must give us at least 2^N, the number of all vectors in our space:

Theorem 4 (sphere covering bound). *If $COV(\rho, N, n)$ exists, then*

$$\sum_{i=0}^{\rho} \binom{N}{i} \geq 2^n.$$

As a trivial example, Theorem 4 tells us that $COV(1, N, n)$ can exist only if $N \geq 2^n - 1$. This shows that covering functions constructed from Hamming codes (Theorem 2) reach this bound. Thus, the associated steganographic schemes are optimal in the following sense. Given $\rho = 1$ and n, the covering function realized using the Hamming code embeds the largest possible relative payload $\alpha = n/N$ (because it has the smallest possible N). The embedding efficiency is $n/\rho = n$. A less trivial example is $COV(3, N, 11)$, where Theorem 4 tells us

$$1 + N + \binom{N}{2} + \binom{N}{3} \geq 2^{11} = 2048.$$

For $N = 23$ we have equality. The corresponding code exists. It is the single most famous code, the binary Golay code. We see that it defines a $COV(3, 23, 11)$, which can embed 11 bits in 23 pixels by at most 3 changes with embedding efficiency $e = 11/3$. The cases when Theorem 4 is satisfied with equality correspond to **perfect codes.** We conclude that the Hamming codes and the binary Golay code are perfect. Unfortunately, the binary Golay code is the only non-trivial binary perfect code with covering radius > 1, so the situation will never be quite as nice again.

We now list several other known families of linear covering functions that provide high embedding efficiency and are thus of interest to the steganographic community. Linear covering functions can be considered from a geometric point of view as well. Consider the linear covering function defined by the check matrix

$$H = \begin{pmatrix} 1\ 0\ 0\ 1 \\ 0\ 1\ 0\ 1 \\ 0\ 0\ 1\ 1 \end{pmatrix}$$

Recalling Theorem 3, since any three-bit message can be obtained by adding at most 2 columns, this check matrix defines a $COV(2,4,3)$. This code is graphically represented in Figure 1 by viewing the black dots as pixels and the attached labels as messages. Notice that any three-bit message can be obtained by adding at most 2 labels of the two black dots. The quadrangle consisting of black dots has the property that each of the remaining 3 points is on some line through two of the quadrangle points. Readers familiar with projective geometry may recognize Figure 1 as the **Fano plane** $PG(2,2)$. This special case can be generalized by looking at nonzero bitstrings of length n as points of a $(n-1)$-dimensional projective geometry $PG(n-1,2)$ defined over $\mathbb{F}_2$. In this language, a linear $COV(2,N,n)$ is equivalent with a set K of N points in $PG(n-1,2)$ having the

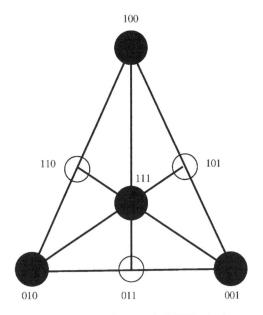

Fig. 1. Fano plane and $COV(2,4,3)$

property that each point of $PG(n-1,2)$ is on a line containing 2 points of K. The family of linear covering functions $COV(2, N, n)$ for $n \leq 7$ and minimal N has been completely classified in Davydov-Marcugini-Pambianco [10].

A family of linear covering functions with covering radius 2, which often yields the best known values, was constructed in Gabidulin-Davydov-Tombak [16] (GDT):

$$COV(2, 5 \cdot 2^{a-1} - 1, 2a + 1) \text{ for } a \geq 1. \tag{1}$$

The smallest member of the family is the $COV(2, 4, 3)$, which we just constructed in the Fano plane. The next parameters are

$$COV(2, 9, 5), \ COV(2, 19, 7), \ COV(2, 39, 9), \ COV(2, 79, 11).$$

The Hamming code H_m $(m \geq 3)$ is known to have a subcode B_m of codimension m within H_m (a **primitive BCH-code**), which has covering radius 3. The corresponding parameters as a covering function are therefore

$$COV(3, 2^m - 1, 2m) \text{ for } m \geq 3. \tag{2}$$

The comparison of embedding efficiency of steganographic schemes based on the linear coverings is compared to best non-linear constructions in Section 7.

4   The Blockwise Direct Sum

In this section, we introduce a recursive procedure called the **blockwise direct sum** BDS of non-linear codes. This very useful tool for constructing coverings is of great interest to us because it can give us covering functions leading to steganographic schemes with higher embedding efficiency than linear covering functions. In fact, virtually all known interesting constructions of coverings make use of it. Although the material in this and the next section is mathematically rather involved, it is mostly self-contained and accessible with only elementary knowledge of coding theory.

In order to apply the BDS, we need a refinement of the concept of a partition of the ambient space into subcodes:

Definition 3. *Let $\mathcal{D} \subset \mathcal{C} \subset \mathbb{F}_2^N$. We say that $\mathcal{C}/\mathcal{D}$ is a **factorization** if $\mathcal{C}$ can be written as the disjoint union of cosets of $\mathcal{D}$ and $\mathbb{F}_2^N$ is a disjoint union of cosets of $\mathcal{C}$.*

Here a coset of $\mathcal{D}$ is a set of the form $\mathcal{D} + x$, in other words a translate. The number of participating cosets of $\mathcal{D}$ in $\mathcal{C}$ is of course $|\mathcal{C}|/|\mathcal{D}|$, the **index** of $\mathcal{D}$ in $\mathcal{C}$. In all cases that we consider, the index will have the form 2^n. We define n to be the **dimension** of $\mathcal{C}/\mathcal{D}$ (or **codimension** of $\mathcal{D}$ in $\mathcal{C}$) in these cases. The **redundancy** k of $\mathcal{C}/\mathcal{D}$ is defined as the redundancy of $\mathcal{C}$, its codimension in the ambient space. We will write U for the ambient space. Observe that whenever two **linear** codes form a chain, e.g., $\mathcal{D} \subset \mathcal{C}$, then they form a factorization. The **length** is the dimension of ambient space.

As an example, consider the factorization U/H_m, where H_m is the Hamming code. The length is $2^m - 1$, we have $dim(U/H_m) = m$ and the redundancy is 0 because the larger of the chain of codes is the ambient space. In general, factorizations of redundancy 0 are precisely covering functions. We need a notion which applies to factorizations and generalizes the covering radius (see Honkala [20]):

Definition 4. *Let C/D be a factorization. For every x in the ambient space let $m(x)$ be the minimum of the distances from x to one of the cosets and $M(x)$ the maximum. The* **norm** $\nu = \nu(C/D)$ *is the maximum, taken over all x, of $m(x) + M(x)$.*

In order to get a feeling for this notion, consider the case when $C = U$. Then each $x \in U$ is contained in one of the cosets defining the factorization. It follows $m(x) = 0$. The norm is therefore the maximum of the $M(x)$. As all cosets of D have the same structure, in particular the same covering radius, it follows that the norm simply equals the covering radius ρ of D. To sum this up: a factorization U/D is nothing but a $COV(\rho, N, n)$, where N is the length, $n = dim(U/D)$ and $\rho = \nu(U/D)$ is the norm.

The BDS is a simple and effective construction which uses as input two factorizations of equal dimension and outputs a factorization of larger length. This is relevant to our problem as we can control the covering radius of the output factorization in terms of the norms of the input.

Definition 5. *Let C_1/D_1 and C_2/D_2 be factorizations of lengths N_i and equal dimension n. Number the participating cosets $D_1(i)$ and $D_2(i)$ for $i = 1, \ldots, 2^n$. The blockwise direct sum $(C_1/D_1) \vee (C_2/D_2)$ is defined by*

$$C = \cup_{i=1}^{2^n} D_1(i) \times D_2(i).$$

The length of the BDS is the sum $N_1 + N_2$ of the lengths and $(C_1 \times C_2)/C$ is a factorization, again of dimension n. The BDS is well-known in the theory of error-correcting codes. It can be used to construct codes with large minimum distance. For the theory of covering codes, it seems to be indispensible. We just convinced ourselves that it works well on the level of factorizations. The main point is that we can control the covering radius:

Theorem 5. *Let C be the blockwise direct sum of two factorizations with identical dimension n, lengths N_i, norms ν_i and redundancies k_i, as in Definition 5. Then C has length $N_1 + N_2$ and redundancy $k_1 + k_2 + n$. The covering radius of C satisfies*

$$\rho(C) \le \lfloor (\nu_1 + \nu_2)/2 \rfloor.$$

Proof. The number of elements of C is obvious. Let (x, y) in the ambient space. Choose j, k such that $d(x, D_1(j))$ and $d(y, D_2(k))$ are minimal. It follows from the definition of the norm that the sum of the distances from (x, y) to $D_1(j) \times D_2(j)$ and to $D_1(k) \times D_2(k)$ is at most $\nu_1 + \nu_2$. One of the two distances must be $\le (\nu_1 + \nu_2)/2$.

Let us express the concepts of a factorization and of the BDS in terms of covering functions. The factorization in the terminology of Definition 3 is equivalently described by a mapping $f = (f_l, f_r) : \mathbb{F}_2^N \longrightarrow \mathbb{F}_2^{k+n}$ where $f_l(x) \in \mathbb{F}_2^k$, $f_r(x) \in \mathbb{F}_2^n$, $f^{-1}(0,0) = \mathcal{D}$, each $f^{-1}(a,b)$ is a coset of $\mathcal{D}$ and $\mathcal{C}$ is the union of the $f^{-1}(0,b)$.

If $f_1 = (f_{1,l}, f_{1,r})$ and $f_2 = (f_{2,l}, f_{2,r})$ describe the factorizations $\mathcal{C}_1/\mathcal{D}_1$ and $\mathcal{C}_2/\mathcal{D}_2$ in Definition 5, then the BDS is defined by

$$(f_1 \vee f_2)(x,y) = (f_{1,l}(x), f_{2,l}(y), f_{1,r}(x) + f_{2,r}(y)) \in \mathbb{F}_2^{k_1+k_2+n}. \tag{3}$$

All we need in order to put the BDS to work are good factorizations to use as inputs. It turns out that a famous family of non-linear codes, the Preparata codes, are extremely valuable ingredients for this machinery.

5   Some Families of Good Factorizations

We know that each $COV(\rho, N, n)$ is nothing but a factorization of redundancy 0, length N and dimension n. It can therefore itself be used as ingredient in the BDS. A factorization we know from Section 3 is H_m/B_m, of length $2^m - 1$, dimension m and redundancy m. The norm is clearly ≤ 4 as H_m has covering radius 1 and B_m has covering radius 3.

An important non-linear factorization is furnished by a famous family of non-linear codes, the Preparata codes. Codes with their parameters were first constructed by Preparata [25], where the reader can find the proof of the following theorem:

Theorem 6. *For every even $m \geq 4$ there is a subcode $P_m \subset H_m$ such that H_m/P_m is a factorization of dimension $m - 1$ and norm 3. More precisely we have that the covering radius of P_m is 3 and that every vector $x \notin H_m$ has distance at most 2 from P_m.*

The factorization of Theorem 6 is the most important non-linear ingredient in constructions of covering codes and covering functions [19]. The smallest member P_4 of the Preparata family was constructed in 1967 [23]. We denote its extension $\overline{P}_4$ by $\mathcal{NR}$ (for the notion of an extension see the paragraph preceding Table 5 below where some elementary facts are explained). This is the famous Nordstrom-Robinson code. It is also the smallest member of the **Kerdock codes**, a family of non-linear codes closely related to the Preparata codes. The Nordstrom-Robinson code has an unusually large group of automorphisms (of order $8! = 40,320$) and is optimal in many respects. It can be found inside the binary Golay code. No linear codes with similar properties as $\mathcal{NR}$ can exist. There are numerous links from the Preparata and Kerdock codes to other mathematical areas, such as finite geometries and group theory. It had been observed early on that the Preparata and Kerdock codes behave like pairs of binary linear codes related by duality, which sounds strange as they are not linear. An explanation for this phenomenon was given in [19]. There are families of linear codes defined over the alphabet $Z_4 = \mathbb{Z}/4\mathbb{Z}$, the integers mod 4, which map to the Preparata and Kerdock codes under the Gray map γ. The Gray map takes $0 \in Z_4$ to 00, the zero-divisor 2 to the pair 11 and the units $1, 3 \in Z_4$ to the pairs of weight 1. It is the only non-linear element in the construction. The original observation that the Preparata and Kerdock codes behave almost as if they were dual linear codes is explained by the fact that their preimages under γ are in fact dual Z_4-linear codes. The same feature explains why H_m/P_m is a factorization. An explicit proof is in Wan's book *Quaternary codes* [31].

In order to understand the factorizations given in the following table, we recall some elementary facts and constructions. The **sum zero code** consists of the bitstrings of even weight. It has codimension 1 in ambient space, being the dual of the repetition code. We denote it by A. In algebra it is also known as the augmentation ideal. If C is a code of length N then its **extension** $\overline{C}$ has length $N + 1$. It has the same number of codewords as C and is defined such that it is contained in the sum zero code A of length $N + 1$. If C/D is a factorization, then $\overline{C}/\overline{D}$ is a factorization as well. Let ν be the norm of C/D. The norm of $\overline{C}/\overline{D}$ is then the even number among $\{\nu + 1, \nu + 2\}$. We arrive at the following list of factorizations.

Some factorizations				
factorization	length	dim	red	norm
U/H_m	$2^m - 1$	m	0	1
$U/\overline{H}_m$	2^m	$m + 1$	0	2
$A/\overline{H}_m$	2^m	m	1	2
H_m/B_m	$2^m - 1$	m	m	4
U/GDT_m	$5 \cdot 2^{m-1} - 1$	$2m + 1$	0	2
H_m/P_m	$2^m - 1$	$m - 1$	m	3
U/P_m	$2^m - 1$	$2m - 1$	0	3
$\overline{H}_m/\overline{P}_m$	2^m	$m - 1$	$m + 1$	4
$U/\overline{P}_m$	2^m	$2m$	0	4
$A/\overline{P}_m$	2^m	$2m - 1$	1	4

Here m has to be even and ≥ 4 whenever P_m is involved. Recall that H_m are the Hamming codes, B_m is the BCH-code introduced in Section 3, and GDT_m is the code from [16] mentioned in the same section.

6   The Best Known Covering Functions

We now give examples of some of the best known covering functions based on the factorizations given in the table at the end of the preceding section. They are included here as a concise summary of the best tools the coding theory currently provides to steganographers for construction of embedding schemes with high embedding efficiency. Their performance is displayed graphically in Section 7. For practitioners, we give a detailed description of the embedding and extraction algorithm for one selected non-linear covering function in Section 8.

The examples below are from Etzion-Greenberg [11] and from Struik's dissertation [30]. Observe that the BDS can be constructed whenever we have factorizations of equal dimension.

Application to H_m/P_m and $A/\overline{H}_{m-1}$ (both of dimension $m-1$) yields, with $m = 2a$,

$$COV(2, 6 \cdot 4^{a-1} - 1, 4a), \ a \geq 2. \tag{4}$$

The first members of this family are

$$COV(2, 23, 8), \ COV(2, 95, 12), \ COV(2, 383, 16), \ COV(2, 1535, 20).$$

The pair U/GDT_m and H_{2m+2}/P_{2m+2} yields

$$COV(2, 4^{m+1} + 5 \cdot 2^{m-1} - 2, 4m + 3) \text{ for } m \geq 1. \tag{5}$$

The first members of this family are

$$COV(2, 19, 7), \ COV(2, 72, 11), \ COV(2, 274, 15), \ COV(2, 1062, 19).$$

As both H_m/P_m and $\overline{H}_m/\overline{P}_m$ have dimension $m-1$, we can form the BDS. It has length $2^m - 1 + 2^m$, redundancy $m + (m-1) + (m+1) = 3m$ and covering radius 3. Let $m = 2a$. This yields

$$COV(3, 2 \cdot 4^a - 1, 6a), \ a \geq 2. \tag{6}$$

The smallest examples are

$$COV(3, 31, 12), \ COV(3, 127, 18) \text{ and } COV(3, 511, 24).$$

These BDS can also be used as ingredients. In fact,

$$(H_m/P_m) \vee (\overline{H}_m/\overline{P}_m) \subset H_m \times (H_m \times \mathbb{F}_2),$$

and this pair forms a factorization of dimension m and norm $3 + 2 = 5$. This gives us the following two additional factorizations to complement Table 5 where $m = 2a \geq 4$:

factorization	length	dim	red	norm
above	$2^{m+1} - 1$	m	$2m$	5
extension	2^{m+1}	m	$2m+1$	6

Using as second ingredient $A/\overline{H}_m$ and forming the BDS, we obtain, with $m = 2a$, the family

$$COV(3, 3 \cdot 4^a - 1, 6a + 1) \text{ for } a \geq 2, \tag{7}$$

whose smallest members are

$$COV(3, 47, 13), \ COV(3, 191, 19), \ COV(3, 767, 25).$$

Forming the BDS of both table entries instead yields, with $m = 2a$,

$$COV(5, 4^{a+1} - 1, 10a + 1) \text{ for } a \geq 2, \tag{8}$$

with the following smallest members

$$COV(5, 63, 21) \text{ and } COV(5, 255, 31).$$

The BDS of H_m/P_m and H_{m-1}/B_{m-1} yields a covering function of length $2^m - 1 + 2^{m-1} - 1$, covering radius 3 and redundancy $3m - 1$. Letting $m = 2(a + 1)$, this becomes

$$COV(3, 6 \cdot 4^a - 2, 6a + 4) \text{ for } a \geq 1, \tag{9}$$

with the smallest members

$$COV(3, 22, 10), \ COV(3, 94, 16), \ COV(3, 382, 22).$$

Finally, we use the direct sum construction of Proposition 1. As an example, the direct sum of the binary Golay code $COV(3, 23, 11)$ and the non-linear $COV(2, 23, 8)$ yields

$$COV(5, 46, 19). \tag{10}$$

7   Performance

Having derived some families of good covering codes, we now study the embedding efficiency that these codes offer to steganographers. As explained in the introduction, an important concept in steganography is the embedding efficiency, which is defined as the ratio between the number of embedded bits and the number of embedding changes. Using the notation $COV(\rho, N, n)$ for the covering function, we remind the terminology from Section 2 where we called the ratio $\alpha = n/N$ the **relative capacity** and $e = n/\rho$ the **embedding efficiency** (in bits per embedding change).

In Figure 2, we show the embedding efficiency as a function of $1/\alpha$ for the binary Hamming code, the binary Golay code, and the families (1)–(10). The upper bound on e for a fixed α can be obtained from the sphere-covering bound (see, e.g., [13])

$$e \leq \frac{\alpha}{H^{-1}(\alpha)}, \tag{11}$$

where $H^{-1}(\alpha)$ is the inverse of the binary entropy function $H(x) = -x \log_2 x - (1 - x) \log_2(1 - x)$ on the interval $[0, 1/2]$. Observe that the recursive constructions of Proposition 1 imply that each $COV(\rho, N, n)$ gives us constructions not only of its asymptotic parameters $(N/n, n/\rho)$ but of an infinite set of such parameter pairs that is dense in the region to the right and down of $(N/n, n/\rho)$. This observation is important for practical applications in steganography – the sender should choose the covering code with relative capacity α slightly above the relative message length that he wants to communicate to the recipient.

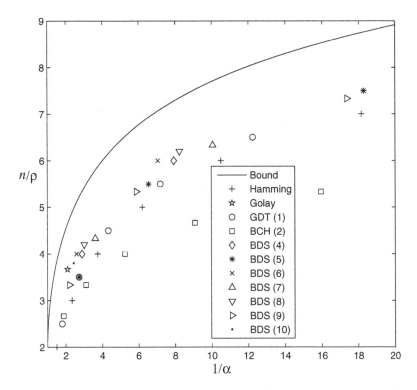

Fig. 2. Embedding efficiency n/ρ as a function of $1/\alpha$ for various covering functions $COV(\rho, N, n)$

Members of the family (6) and (8) lead to the highest embedding efficiency, providing significant improvement over the simple binary Hamming codes.

Observe that since the covering radius ρ gives a bound on the average number of embedding changes ρ_a, the embedding efficiency as defined in this paper is a lower bound on the embedding effiency n/ρ_a as typically defined in steganographic literature. From our perspective, it is preferable to work with a simple invariant like ρ. The situation is analogous to the classical coding theory scenario where in most situations the minimum distance d, rather than the average distance, is used to obtain bounds on the error probability. Actually, the difference $n/\rho_a - e$ is small and goes to 0 with increasing length.

The last issue that needs to be addressed for practical applications is the implementation complexity. This is the topic of the next section where we discuss implementation details for the family of codes (4), as an example.

8   Implementation

In this section, we describe in detail the embedding algorithm and the algorithm for extracting the secret message bits based on the covering codes (4) for $m = 4$

(the covering function $COV(2, 23, 8)$). We start by detailing the factorizations H_m/P_m, $A/\overline{H}_{m-1}$ and their covering functions.

8.1 The Factorization H_4/P_4 and Its Covering Function

Start with a description of the Nordstrom-Robinson code $\mathcal{NR} = \overline{P}_4$. This is a binary code of length 16, with 2^8 codewords, minimum distance 6 and covering radius 4. It is the smallest member of the Preparata family and the single most famous non-linear code. Among its exceptional properties is the presence of a huge group of symmetries, of order 8! For an introduction see [3]. As mentioned earlier, the charm of the Preparata codes is that they are essentially linear over Z_4. This means that there is an underlying code, which is linear over Z_4, and the binary code in question is the image of this Z_4-linear code under the Gray map γ, where

$$\gamma: \ 0 \mapsto 00, \ 1 \mapsto 10, \ 3 \mapsto 01, \ 2 \mapsto 11.$$

In order to construct the Nordstrom-Robinson code start from the binary matrix

$$\begin{pmatrix} 1000 & 0111 \\ 0100 & 1011 \\ 0010 & 1101 \\ 0001 & 1110 \end{pmatrix}, \tag{12}$$

which generates the extended Hamming code $[8, 4, 4]_2$ (length 8, dimension 4, minimum distance 4). As this code is equal to its orthogonal with respect to the ordinary dot product (it is self-dual) it is tempting to lift this matrix to a matrix with entries in Z_4. Observe that the factor ring of Z_4 mod $\{0, 2\}$ is the binary field $\mathbb{F}_2$. Lifting means that each entry $0 \in \mathbb{F}_2$ should become 0 or 2 in Z_4 and each $1 \in \mathbb{F}_2$ should be replaced by 1 or 3 in Z_4. We want the lift to have the property that it is self-dual over Z_4. After a moment's thought this leads to the matrix

$$G = (I|P) = \begin{pmatrix} 1000 & 2333 \\ 0100 & 1231 \\ 0010 & 1123 \\ 0001 & 1312 \end{pmatrix}.$$

The self-dual Z_4-linear code generated by the rows of this matrix is known as the **octacode** $\mathcal{N}$. The Nordstrom-Robinson code is its image under the Gray map: $\mathcal{NR} = \overline{P}_4 = \gamma(\mathcal{N})$. The length and number of codewords are as promised and it is not hard to check that the minimum distance and covering radius are as claimed. The codewords of $\mathcal{N}$ are $x(a, b, c, d) = (l|r)$ where $l = (a, b, c, d)$, $a, b, c, d \in Z_4$. and

$$r = s(l) = (2a + b + c + d, -a + 2b + c - d, -a - b + 2c + d, -a + b - c + 2d).$$

The proof of the following lemma can be left as an easy exercise, using the self-duality of $\mathcal{N}$.

Lemma 1. *Let $x \in \mathcal{N}$ and $\nu_i(x)$ for $i \in Z_4$ the frequency of i as an entry of x. Then the $\nu_i(x)$ have the same parity.*

In order to see that $U/\mathcal{NR}$ is a factorization, observe that $\mathcal{N}$ is **systematic:** in the projection on the left half of parameters each quaternary quadruple occurs precisely once. It follows that the binary code $\mathcal{NR}$ is systematic as well: in the projection on the left half of parameters each binary 8-tuple occurs precisely once. Systematic codes can always be embedded in factorizations. In fact, the $(0, y)$, where $y \in Z_4^4$ are representatives of pairwise disjoint cosets of $\mathcal{N}$. The union of those cosets is the ambient space $U = Z_4^8$. It follows that the same is true for $\mathcal{NR}$. The codewords of $\mathcal{NR}$ are $(\gamma(l), \gamma(s(l)))$, where $l \in Z_4^4$. Write $(x, y) \in \mathbb{F}_2^{8+8}$ as

$$(x, y) = (\gamma(l), y) = (\gamma(l), \gamma(s(l))) + (0, y + \gamma(s(l))).$$

This decomposition enables us to formulate the following proposition.

Proposition 2. *A $COV(4, 16, 8)$ corresponding to the factorization $\mathbb{F}_2^{16}/\mathcal{NR}$ is given by*

$$f(x, y) = y + \gamma(s(\gamma^{-1}(x))).$$

Here $x, y \in \mathbb{F}_2^8$.

As an example, consider $(x, y) = (00100111, 10011001)$. Then $\gamma^{-1}(x) = 0132$, $s(0132) = 2332$, $\gamma(2332) = 11010111$ and

$$f(x, y) = 10011001 + 11010111 = 01001110.$$

The observation that systematic codes can be embedded in factorizations is from Stinson [29], where a characterization of resilient functions is given in terms of factorizations.

The factorization $U/\mathcal{NR}$ itself is not an interesting covering function. It yields good results when used as an ingredient in the BDS. We mentioned and used a factorization $\overline{H}_4/\mathcal{NR}$ of length 16, dimension 3 and redundancy 5. Here $\overline{H}_4$ is the extended Hamming code, a linear $[16, 11, 4]$-code. At first we have to see that $\mathcal{NR}$ is in fact contained in the Hamming code. Let

$$G = \begin{pmatrix} 11000000 & 00111111 \\ 00110000 & 11001111 \\ 00001100 & 11110011 \\ 00000011 & 11111100 \\ 01010101 & 01010101 \end{pmatrix}.$$

This is a check matrix of the extended Hamming code $\overline{H}_4 = [16, 11, 4]_2$ (equivalently: no 3 columns of G add to the 0-column). It is orthogonal to all codewords of $\mathcal{NR}$ (for the first 4 rows of G this is obvious, for the last row use Lemma 1). It follows $\mathcal{NR} \subset \overline{H}_4$. Let

$$T = \langle \gamma(2200), \gamma(2020), \gamma(2002) \rangle.$$

Then $(0, T) \subset \overline{H}_4$ as those vectors are orthogonal to the rows of G. The first half of coordinates shows that the cosets $\mathcal{NR} + (0, t)$, $t \in T$ are pairwise disjoint. This defines a factorization $\overline{H}_4 / \mathcal{NR}$.

Let us calculate the covering function $f = (f_1, f_2) : \mathbb{F}_2^{16} \longrightarrow \mathbb{F}_2^8$ which describes the factorization $\overline{H}_4 / \mathcal{NR}$. Let $r_i, i = 1, \dots, 5$ be the rows and $s_j, j = 1, \dots, 16$ the columns of G. Let $z = (x|y) \in \mathbb{F}_2^{8+8}$ and denote by e_i the elementary vectors. The first section simply is the syndrome:

$$f_1(z) = (z \cdot r_1, z \cdot r_2, z \cdot r_3, z \cdot r_4, z \cdot r_5) = (\sigma | z \cdot r_5) \in \mathbb{F}_2^{4+1}.$$

Let the $\mathbb{F}_2$-linear mapping $\beta : T \longrightarrow \langle e_6, e_7, e_8 \rangle$ be defined by

$$\beta(\gamma(2200)) = e_6, \quad \beta(\gamma(2020)) = e_7, \quad \beta(\gamma(2002)) = e_8.$$

In order to calculate f_2, proceed as follows:

- If σ has odd weight, then $f_1(z) = s_j$ is a column of G. Let $z' = z + e_j, \gamma^{-1}(z') = (l, r)$. Then $\gamma(r - s(l)) = (0, t)$ for $t \in T$. Let $f_2(z) = \beta(t)$.
- If σ has even weight, then $f_1(z) = s_1 + s_j$ for a uniquely determined column s_j of G. Let $z' = z + e_1 + e_j$ and continue as in the preceding case.

As an example, consider $z = 11001001|00011001$. The syndrome is the sum of columns number $1, 2, 5, 8, 12, 13, 16$ of G:

$$f_1(z) = 10110.$$

As $\sigma = 1011$ has weight 3, we have that $f_1(z) = s_{11}$ is a column of G. It follows $z' = 11001001|00111001 \in \overline{H}_4$. Then

$$l = 2013, \ r = 0213, \ s(l) = 0033, r - s(l) = 0220 \in \gamma^{-1}(0, T)$$

as promised. Applying γ and β yields $f_2(z) = e_6 + e_7$:

$$f(z) = (f_1(z)|f_2(z)) = 10110|110.$$

This can be adapted to obtain the covering function g describing the factorization H_4 / P_4 of the shortened codes: Let $z \in \mathbb{F}_2^{15}$. Add a parity check bit in the beginning to obtain $z' \in \mathbb{F}_2^{16}$ of even weight. Then

$$g(z) = (g_1(z)|g_2(z)) = (z' \cdot r_2, z' \cdot r_3, z' \cdot r_4, z' \cdot r_5 | f_2(z')) \in \mathbb{F}_2^{4+3}.$$

This function $g = (g_1, g_2)$ is the covering function of the first factorization H_4 / P_4 and constitutes the first ingredient in the construction of $COV(2, 23, 8)$ (family (4) in the beginning of Section 6). To give an example of how the function works, let $z = 11000001|0001100$. Then $z' = 11000001|00011001$. Application of f as before yields $f(z') = 10010|011$. Now $g(z)$ is obtained by removing the first bit:

$$g(z) = 0010|011.$$

8.2 The Factorization $A/\overline{H}_3$ and Its Covering Function

This factorization has length 8 and dimension 3. Here $\overline{H}_3$ is the extended Hamming code $[8, 4, 4]_2$ again. Using its generator matrix as given in the beginning of the present section, we can write the corresponding covering function as $h(y) = (h_1(y), h_2(y))$, where $y \in \mathbb{F}_2^8$ and

$$h_1(y) = y_1 + \cdots + y_8, \quad h_2(y) = (y_1 + y_6 + y_7 + y_8,$$

$$y_2 + y_5 + y_7 + y_8, \quad y_3 + y_5 + y_6 + y_8).$$

8.3 Message Extraction Algorithm

We are now ready to describe the algorithm using which the recipient can extract the secret message. Since we are using a covering $COV(2, 23, 8)$, we extract 8 secret message bits from a block of 23 pixels.

Using (3), the covering function of a $COV(2, 23, 8)$ is $g \vee h$, concretely

$$(g \vee h)(x, y) = (g_1(x), h_1(y), g_2(x) + h_2(y)) \in \mathbb{F}_2^8,$$

where, of course, $x \in \mathbb{F}_2^{15}$, $y \in \mathbb{F}_2^8$.

To complete the description of the steganographic scheme, we need to explain the embedding mechanism.

8.4 Message Embedding Algorithm

Here, we describe the action of the embedder whose task is to hide 8 message bits in a cover image block consisting of 23 pixels by modifying at most 2 LSBs. Let $(x, y) \in \mathbb{F}_2^{15+8}$ be given such that $f(x, y) = (g \vee h)(x, y) = (a, b, c) \in \mathbb{F}_2^{4+1+3}$ and let $(A, B, C) \in \mathbb{F}_2^{4+1+3}$ be the section of the secret message that we wish to embed. We need to describe how to change (x, y) in at most 2 coordinates such that the resulting bitstring is mapped to (A, B, C). Naturally, we use matrix G above and its submatrix G' obtained by omitting the first row of G. The linear mapping h is based on matrix

$$H = \begin{pmatrix} 11111111 \\ 10000111 \\ 01001011 \\ 00101101 \end{pmatrix}.$$

Observe that the columns of G' are all quadruples, starting with the 0 quadruple and the columns of H are all quadruples that start with 1. We can describe the embedding procedure. Number the columns of G' from 0 to 15, those of H from 1 to 8.

- Assume $b + B = 1, A = a$. Let $(1, c + C)$ be column number j of H. Change bit number j of y, leave x unchanged.
- Assume $b + B = 1, A \neq a$. Choose j as above and choose $i \leq 15$ such that $a + A$ is column i of G'. Change the i-th bit of x and the j-th bit of y.
- Let $B = b, A = a$. Change y in two coordinates j_1 and j_2 such that the corresponding columns of H add to $(0, c + C)$.
- Let $B = b, A \neq a$. Consider the 8 pairs of columns of G' that add to $A + a$. This corresponds to 7 vectors $x'_1, \ldots, x'_7$ at distance 2 from x and one vector x'_8 at distance 1 (the corresponding column of G' being $A = a$). The values $g_2(x'_i)$ are all different. Choose i such that $g_2(x'_i) + g_2(x) = C + c$.

This completes the description of a steganographic scheme based on family (4) for $m = 4$, or $COV(2, 23, 8)$.

9 Conclusion

In this paper, we show that certain families of non-linear codes can achieve markedly better performance (higher embedding efficiency) for applications in steganography than simple linear codes currently in use. We construct the codes using the blockwise direct sum of code factorizations. For practitioners, we provide a detailed description of one selected family of covering functions.

The smallest open problem in constructing good families of coverings is the existence of $COV(2, 12, 6)$. A more general problem is to use the known families of good Z_4-linear codes for the construction of covering codes and covering functions. An even more ambitious aim is to bring algebraic-geometric codes into play. Finally, the theory of covering functions should not be restricted to the binary case.

References

1. Bierbrauer, J.: Introduction to Coding Theory. Chapman and Hall, CRC Press (2005)
2. Bierbrauer, J.: Crandall's problem (unpublished, 1998), available from, http://www.ws.binghamton.edu/fridrich/covcodes.pdf
3. Bierbrauer, J.: Nordstrom-Robinson code and A_7-geometry. Finite Fields and Their Applications 13, 158–170 (2007)
4. Cachin, C.: An information-theoretic model for steganography. In: Aucsmith, D. (ed.) IH 1998. LNCS, vol. 1525, pp. 306–318. Springer, Heidelberg (1998)
5. Carnielli, W.A.: On covering and coloring problems for rook domains. Discrete Mathematics 57, 9–16 (1985)
6. Cohen, G., Honkala, I., Litsyn, S., Lobstein, A.: Covering Codes. North Holland, Amsterdam (1997)
7. Crandall, R.: Some notes on steganography. Posted on steganography mailing list (1998), http://os.inf.tu-dresden.de/~westfeld/crandall.pdf
8. Davydov, A.A.: New constructions of covering codes. Designs, Codes and Cryptography 22, 305–316 (2001)

9. Davydov, A.A., Faina, G., Marcugini, S., Pambianco, F.: Locally optimal (non-shortening) linear covering codes and minimal saturating sets in projective spaces. IEEE Transactions on Information Theory 51, 4378–4387 (2005)

10. Davydov, A.A., Marcugini, S., Pambianco, F.: Minimal 1 -saturating sets and complete caps in binary projective spaces. Journal of Combinatorial Theory A 113, 647–663 (2006)

11. Etzion, T., Greenberg, G.: Constructions for perfect mixed codes and other covering codes. IEEE Transactions on Information Theory 39, 209–214 (1993)

12. Etzion, T., Mounits, B.: Quasi-perfect codes with small distance. IEEE Transactions on Information Theory 51, 3938–3946 (2005)

13. Fridrich, J., Goljan, M., Soukal, D.: Efficient Wet Paper Codes. In: Barni, M., Herrera-Joancomartí, J., Katzenbeisser, S., Pérez-González, F. (eds.) IH 2005. LNCS, vol. 3727, pp. 204–218. Springer, Heidelberg (2005)

14. Fridrich, J.: Feature-Based Steganalysis for JPEG Images and its Implications for Future Design of Steganographic Schemes. In: Fridrich, J. (ed.) IH 2004. LNCS, vol. 3200, pp. 67–81. Springer, Heidelberg (2004)

15. Fridrich, J., Goljan, M., Du, R.: Steganalysis Based on JPEG Compatibility. In: Tescher, et al. (eds.) Proc. SPIE Multimedia Systems and Applications IV, SPIE, vol. 4518, Denver, CO. pp. 275–280 (August 2001)

16. Gabidulin, E.M., Davydov, A.A., Tombak, I.M.: Codes with covering radius 2 and other new covering codes. IEEE Transactions on Information Theory 37, 219–224 (1991)

17. Galand, F., Kabatiansky, G.: Information hiding by coverings. In: Proceedings of the IEEE Information Theory Workshop 2004, pp. 151–154 (2004)

18. Goppa, V.D.: Codes on algebraic curves. Soviet Math. Doklady 24, 170–172 (1981)

19. Hammons Jr, A.R., Kumar, P.V., Calderbank, A.R., Sloane, N.J.A., Solé, P.: The Z_4-linearity of Kerdock, Preparata, Goethals and related codes. IEEE Transactions on Information Theory 40, 301–319 (1994)

20. Honkala, I.S.: On (k, t)-subnormal covering codes. IEEE Transactions on Information Theory 37, 1203–1206 (1991)

21. Kaikkonen, M.K., Rosendahl, P.: New covering codes from an ADS-like construction. IEEE Transactions on Information Theory 49, 1809–1812 (2003)

22. Ker, A.: A General Framework for Structural Analysis of LSB Replacement. In: Barni, M., Herrera-Joancomartí, J., Katzenbeisser, S., Pérez-González, F. (eds.) IH 2005. LNCS, vol. 3727, pp. 296–311. Springer, Heidelberg (2005)

23. Nordstrom, A.W., Robinson, J.P.: An optimum nonlinear code. Information and Control 11, 613–616 (1967)

24. Östergå, P.: A coloring problem in Hamming spaces. European Journal of Combinatorics 18, 303–309 (1997)

25. Preparata, F.P.: A class of optimum nonlinear double-error-correcting codes. Information and Control 13, 378–400 (1968)

26. Provos, N.: Defending Against Statistical Steganalysis. In: 10th USENIX Security Symposium, Washington, DC (2001)

27. Sallee, P.: Model Based Steganography. In: Kalker, T., Cox, I., Ro, Y.M. (eds.) IWDW 2003. LNCS, vol. 2939, pp. 154–167. Springer, Heidelberg (2004)

28. Simmons, G.J.: The Prisoners' Problem and the Subliminal Channel. In: Chaum, D. (ed.) Advances in Cryptology: Proceedings of Crypto 1983, pp. 51–67. Plenum Press (1984)

29. Stinson, D.R.: Resilient functions and large sets of orthogonal arrays. Congressus Numerantium 92, 105–110 (1993)
30. Struik, R.: Covering Codes, Ph.D. dissertation, Eindhoven (1994)
31. Wan, Z.X.: Quaternary codes. World Scientific, Singapore (1997)
32. Westfeld, A.: High Capacity Despite Better Steganalysis (F5–A Steganographic Algorithm). In: Moskowitz, I.S. (ed.) IH 2001. LNCS, vol. 2137, pp. 289–302. Springer, Heidelberg (2001)
33. Zelinka, B.: On k-domatic numbers of graphs. Czechoslovak Math. Journal 33, 309–311 (1983)

On the Use of Bhattacharyya Distance as a Measure of the Detectability of Steganographic Systems

Valery Korzhik[1], Hideki Imai[2], Junji Shikata[3],
Guillermo Morales-Luna[4,*], and Ekaterina Gerling[1]

[1] State University of Telecommunications, St. Petersburg, Russia
korzhik@spb.lanck.net
[2] Chuo University and National Institute of Advanced Industrial Science and
Technology (AIST), Japan
h-imai@aist.go.jp
[3] Graduate School of Environment and Information Science, Yokohama National
University, Japan
shikata@ynu.ac.jp
[4] Computer Science, CINVESTAV-IPN, Mexico City, Mexico
gmorales@cs.cinvestav.mx

Abstract. It is very common to use the notion of *relative entropy* (or *Kullback-Leibler divergence*) as a measure for the discrimination difficulty among the hypotheses testing of presence and absence within a steganographic system. Relative entropy is not a symmetric function and sometimes it is very hard to compute its values. We propose to customize the notion of *Bhattacharyya distance* to the solution of the same problem. The main properties of Bhattacharyya distance are presented. We show applications of this new steganographic system security criterion within the model with a Gaussian colored covertext and within spread-spectrum watermarking by a white Gaussian sequence.

Keywords: Steganography, Bhattacharyya distance, spread spectrum signal, detectability of stegosystems.

1 Introduction

It is very common to think that a natural way of defining the detectability of a steganographic (SG) system is in terms of *relative entropies* (or *Kullback-Leibler divergence*) $D(P_S\|P_X)$, $D(P_X\|P_S)$, where P_S is the probability distribution on a covertext S and P_X is the probability distribution on a stegotext X (C. Cachin pioneered the use of such criterion for SG systems [1]).

In the case of any two continuous distributions P, Q, the relative entropies can be presented as in [2]

$$D(P\|Q) = \int_{\Omega} P(\omega) \log\left(\frac{P(\omega)}{Q(\omega)}\right) d\omega \qquad (1)$$

where Ω is the space of possible measurements.

* Dr. Morales-Luna acknowledges the support of Mexican Conacyt.

Y.Q. Shi (Ed.): Transactions on DHMS III, LNCS 4920, pp. 23–32, 2008.

The efficiency of hypothesis testing can be characterized by two probabilities: the probability P_m of *missing* (when the stegosignal has been embedded but the detector wrongly declares its absence) and the probability P_{fa} of *false alarm* (when the stegosignal has not been embedded but the detector wrongly declares its presence). A lower bound [3,4] for the Bayesian probability error $P_e = \pi_0 P_{fa} + \pi_1 P_m$, where π_0 and π_1 are priors of the hypotheses, is

$$P_e > \pi_0 \pi_1 \exp\left(-\frac{J}{2}\right)$$

where $J = D(P_S\|P_X) + D(P_X\|P_S)$. It follows from Information Theory [2] that, for any hypothesis testing rule, the following inequalities hold

$$P_{fa} \log\left(\frac{P_{fa}}{1 - P_m}\right) + (1 - P_{fa}) \log\left(\frac{1 - P_{fa}}{P_m}\right) \le D(P_S\|P_X) \qquad (2)$$

$$P_m \log\left(\frac{P_m}{1 - P_{fa}}\right) + (1 - P_m) \log\left(\frac{1 - P_m}{P_{fa}}\right) \le D(P_X\|P_S) \qquad (3)$$

For $P_{fa} = 0$, we get from relation (2), $P_m \ge 2^{-D(P_S\|P_X)}$.

We can see from (2), (3) that the SG system is *unconditionally secure* (or *perfectly undetectable*) if $D(P_S\|P_X) = 0 = D(P_X\|P_S)$. It has been proved [4] that the relative entropies $D(P_S\|P_X), D(P_X\|P_S)$, given by (1), can be calculated for general zero-mean (N-dimensional) Gaussian distributions P_S, P_X, as follows

$$D(P_{X^N}\|P_{S^N}) = -\frac{1}{2} \ln \det(I_N + \delta R) + \frac{1}{2} \operatorname{tr}(\delta R)$$

$$D(P_{S^N}\|P_{X^N}) = -\frac{1}{2} \ln \det\left(I_N + \delta\tilde{R}\right) + \frac{1}{2} \operatorname{tr}(\delta\tilde{R}) \qquad (4)$$

where I_N is the $(N \times N)$-identity matrix, $\operatorname{tr}(\cdot)$ denotes the trace of a matrix, R_{X^N}, R_{S^N} are the covariance matrices of the Gaussian N-dimensional random vectors X^N (stegotext) and S^N (covertext), respectively, and

$$\delta R = R_{X^N} R_{S^N}^{-1} - I_N \quad , \quad \delta\tilde{R} = R_{S^N} R_{X^N}^{-1} - I_N.$$

For a good stegosystem, whenever R_{X^N} is close to R_{S^N}, the parameter J can be accurately approximated [4] by the relation

$$J \approx \frac{1}{2} \operatorname{tr}\left((\delta R)^2\right) \qquad (5)$$

It can be seen from (5) that even for the fortunate case of a "good" stegosystem with Gaussian covertext distribution we will face a serious problem under the calculation of J by (5). Moreover, it has been shown in [5] that the Gaussian distribution is not the case for typical images and then a calculation of relative entropy by (1) poses a very hard problem.

In Section 2 we propose another measure of the detectability of stegosystems based on *Bhattacharyya distance* (BD). We present its properties and explicit forms for some probability distributions. In Section 3 we describe some applications of a new criterion to estimate the security for the stegosystem (SGS) based on additive spread-spectrum watermarking. Section 4 concludes the paper.

2   BD and Its Main Properties

Thomas Kailath pioneered in applying BD to an estimation of the error probability. BD has been effectively used by Kailath [6] as a technique to estimate the probability of error for an optimal receiver under the condition of binary signaling over noisy channel. Later this criterion was used by many researchers in communication theory [7,8]. Accordingly with [6], BD is defined between two probability distributions P_S and P_X over a space Ω as

$$D_B(P_S, P_X) = -\ln \rho_B(P_S, P_X) \qquad (6)$$

where

$$\rho_B(P_S, P_X) = \int_\Omega \sqrt{P_X(\omega)P_S(\omega)}\, d\omega. \qquad (7)$$

From (6), (7), it follows that $D_B(P_S, P_X) = D_B(P_X, P_S)$, thus D_B is a symmetric function, and although it does not satisfy the triangle inequality [6], the slight variant $\sqrt{1 - \rho_B^2}$ does indeed satisfy it. Therefore under this criterion it is not necessary to calculate the two values $D(P_X\|P_S)$ and $D(P_S\|P_X)$ as was the case for the criterion based on relative entropy [4]. (The triangle inequality can be useful in the case of double embedding in different nodes of a computer network, for instance.)

If prior probabilities π_0 and π_1 coincide (e.g. $\pi_0 = \pi_1 = 1/2$) then the Bayesian error probability P_e under the condition of optimal hypothesis testing is bounded [6] as

$$\frac{1}{4}\rho_B^2(P_X, P_S) \leq P_e \leq \frac{1}{2}\rho_B(P_X, P_S) \qquad (8)$$

For the special case $P_X = P_S$ we obtain $\rho_B(P_X, P_S) = 1$ and $D_B(P_X, P_S) = 0$. This means that the SGS is unconditionally secure. We will say that it is ε-secure if $D_B(P_X, P_S) = \varepsilon$. Then in this case,

$$P_e \geq \frac{1}{4}\exp(-2\varepsilon). \qquad (9)$$

Inequality (9) states that if $D_B(P_X, P_S)$ is very close to 0 or $\rho_B(P_X, P_S)$ is very close to 1 then the stegosystem occurs *almost secure*.

If X^N, S^N are N-dimensional Gaussian random vectors then [6]

$$D_B(P_{X^N}, P_{S^N}) = \frac{1}{8}(v_{X^N} - v_{S^N})^T R^{-1}(v_{X^N} - v_{S^N}) +$$
$$\frac{1}{2}\ln \frac{\det R}{\sqrt{\det R_{X^N} \det R_{S^N}}} \qquad (10)$$

where v_{X^N}, v_{S^N} are the mean value vectors and R_{X^N}, R_{S^N} are the covariance matrices of the N-dimensional random vectors X^N, S^N, respectively, the superindex T denotes matrix transposition and $R = \frac{1}{2}(R_{X^N} + R_{S^N})$.

In the particular case when $v_{X^N} = v_{S^N}$ (which holds whenever the vectors X^N, S^N have zero-mean) we get from (10)

$$D_B\left(P_{X^N}, P_{S^N}\right) = \frac{1}{2}\ln\frac{\det R}{\sqrt{\det R_{X^N}\ \det R_{S^N}}}. \tag{11}$$

In another particular case, when $R_{X^N} = R_{S^N} = R$, we get from (10)

$$D_B\left(P_{X^N}, P_{S^N}\right) = \frac{1}{8}\left(v_{X^N} - v_{S^N}\right)^T R^{-1}\left(v_{X^N} - v_{S^N}\right).$$

If the space Ω is discrete-valued, we may rephrase (7) as

$$\rho_B\left(P_{X^N}, P_{S^N}\right) = \sum_{\omega \in \Omega}\sqrt{P_{X^N}(\omega)P_{S^N}(\omega)}.$$

The upper bound in (8) can be improved in general [8] if the modified Bhattacharyya coefficient $\widetilde{\rho}_B\left(P_{X^N}, P_{S^N}\right)$ is used in (6), where

$$\widetilde{\rho}_B\left(P_{X^N}, P_{S^N}\right) = \min_{0 \leq s \leq 1}\int_{\Omega} P_{X^N}^s(\omega)P_{S^N}^{1-s}(\omega)\,d\omega$$

3   Design of an almost Secure SGS Invariant to Covertext Distribution

Let us consider the conventional *spread-spectrum* (SS) embedding in the additive manner

$$X^N = aS^N + W^N \tag{12}$$

where the host signal S^N is a Gaussian random vector with independent identically distributed components, i.e. $S^N \sim N(0, \sigma_S I_N)$ scaled by a, and W^N is also chosen as a Gaussian zero mean i.i.d. random vector with variance σ_W^2. If the coefficient a is chosen as $\alpha = 1 - \frac{D}{2\sigma_S^2}$ and $\sigma_W^2 = D\left(1 - \frac{D}{4\sigma_S^2}\right)$ then the embedding distortion equals D and $D\left(P_{X^N}\|P_{S^N}\right) = 0$ [4]. This means that such SGS is a *perfectly undetectable stegosystem*.

But it is very impractical to model covertext as an i.i.d. random vector. If we assume that S^N is a correlated source then, as it has been proved in [4], a perfectly undetectable SGS can be achieved after an application to S^N of the Karhunen-Loève transform (KLT), an additive scaled embedding(as in (12)) into the KLT coefficients and a recovering of the stegotext by the inverse KLT transform.

However, an application of KLT requires the *knowledge* of the covariance matrix of S^N. Obviously, the number of real images that can appeared as covertext is huge and, even though there exists the average covariance matrix for typical images, it is impossible to take it for performance evaluation of KLT in a particular image.

Let us consider the embedding function in the form (12) for a stegotext with arbitrary probability distribution when D and N are chosen in a such a way that at least an ε-secure SGS can be provided, i.e. with either $D(P_{X^N} \| P_{S^N}) = \varepsilon$ or $D_B(P_{X^N}, P_{S^N}) = \varepsilon$.

In this case the attacker must distinguish between Gaussian noises created by the embedding process from those introduced during the image acquisition itself [5]. Generally, a device noise have non-Gaussian distribution [9] and it requires the use of embedding noise approximating a device noise closely as possible.

We consider in the current paper the model with colored Gaussian covertext and i.i.d. Gaussian embedding noise. The main goal of our investigation is to find out how the correlation of stegotext affects on the security of such SG-systems.

Let us assume that the covariance matrix of the Gaussian covertext S^N is

$$
R_{S^N} = \sigma_S^2
\begin{bmatrix}
1 & r_{12} & \cdots & r_{1,N-1} & r_{1N} \\
r_{21} & 1 & \cdots & r_{2,N-1} & r_{2N} \\
\vdots & \vdots & \ddots & \vdots & \vdots \\
r_{N-1,1} & r_{N-1,2} & \cdots & 1 & r_{N-1,N} \\
r_{N1} & r_{N2} & \cdots & r_{N,N-1} & 1
\end{bmatrix}
$$

where for each $i, j \leq N$, $r_{ij} = \frac{E(S(i)S(j))}{\sigma_S^2}$, and $S(i)$ is the i-th sample of the covertext.

Then it is easy to see that the covariance matrix of the stegotext X^N after the embedding by (12) will be

$$
R_{X^N} = \sigma_S^2 d^{-1}
\begin{bmatrix}
d & r_{12} & \cdots & r_{1,N-1} & r_{1N} \\
r_{21} & d & \cdots & r_{2,N-1} & r_{2N} \\
\vdots & \vdots & \ddots & \vdots & \vdots \\
r_{N-1,1} & r_{N-1,2} & \cdots & d & r_{N-1,N} \\
r_{N1} & r_{N2} & \cdots & r_{N,N-1} & d
\end{bmatrix}
$$

where $d = \left(1 - \frac{D}{2\sigma_S^2}\right)^{-2}$.

In the particular case of exponential correlation, when S^N is an AR(1) zero mean sequence, the following Toeplitz matrix R_{S^N} and "almost-Toeplitz" matrix R_{X^N} result:

$$
R_{S^N} = \sigma_S^2
\begin{bmatrix}
1 & r & \cdots & r^{N-2} & r^{N-1} \\
r & 1 & \cdots & r^{N-3} & r^{N-2} \\
\vdots & \vdots & \ddots & \vdots & \vdots \\
r^{N-2} & r^{N-3} & \cdots & 1 & r \\
r^{N-1} & r^{N-2} & \cdots & r & 1
\end{bmatrix}
$$

$$
R_{X^N} = d^{-1}\sigma_S^2
\begin{bmatrix}
d & r & \cdots & r^{N-2} & r^{N-1} \\
r & d & \cdots & r^{N-3} & r^{N-2} \\
\vdots & \vdots & \ddots & \vdots & \vdots \\
r^{N-2} & r^{N-3} & \cdots & d & r \\
r^{N-1} & r^{N-2} & \cdots & r & d
\end{bmatrix}
\tag{13}
$$

Unfortunately it is not easy to calculate the relative entropy by (4) (and even an approximation by (5)) for these matrices. If we assume the Bhattacharrya distance as a difference measure between the two Gaussian zero mean colored distributions P_{X^N}, P_{S^N} we get, by (6), (8), (11),

$$P_e \geq \frac{1}{4}\rho^2 = \frac{1}{4}\frac{\sqrt{\det R_{X^N}\ \det R_{S^N}}}{\det\left(\frac{1}{2}\left(R_{X^N} + R_{S^N}\right)\right)} \tag{14}$$

where R_{X^N}, R_{S^N} are given in (13). After simple transforms and taking into account (13) we get

$$R = \frac{1}{2}\left(R_{X^N} + R_{S^N}\right) = t\sigma_S^2 \begin{bmatrix} t^{-1} & r & \dots & r^{N-2} & r^{N-1} \\ r & t^{-1} & \dots & r^{N-3} & r^{N-2} \\ \vdots & \vdots & \ddots & \vdots & \vdots \\ r^{N-2} & r^{N-3} & \dots & t^{-1} & r \\ r^{N-1} & r^{N-2} & \dots & r & t^{-1} \end{bmatrix}$$

where $t = \frac{1+d^{-1}}{2}$. The determinant of the Toeplitz matrix R_{S^N} can easily be calculated [10] as

$$\det R_{S^N} = \sigma_S^{2N}(1 - r^2)^{N-1}. \tag{15}$$

For the almost-Toeplitz matrices R_{S^N} and R, their determinants can be found [7] as

$$\det R_{X^N} = \left(d^{-1}\sigma_S^2\right)^N a_N \quad , \quad \det R = \left(t\sigma_S^2\right)^N b_N \tag{16}$$

where the parameters a_N and b_N are calculated through the recurrence formulas

$$\begin{aligned} \alpha_0 &= 1 \\ \alpha_1 &= d + (d-2)r^2 \\ \forall n = 2,\dots,N-1: \quad \alpha_n &= (d + (d-2)r^2)\alpha_{n-1} - ((d-1)r)^2\alpha_{n-2} \\ a_N &= d\alpha_{N-1} - ((d-1)r)^2\alpha_{N-2} \end{aligned} \tag{17}$$

and

$$\begin{aligned} \beta_0 &= 1 \\ \beta_1 &= d_1 + (d_1-2)r^2 \\ \forall n = 2,\dots,N-1: \quad \beta_n &= (d_1 + (d_1-2)r^2)\beta_{n-1} - ((d_1-1)r)^2\beta_{n-2} \\ b_N &= d_1\beta_{N-1} - ((d_1-1)r)^2\beta_{N-2} \end{aligned} \tag{18}$$

with $d_1 = t^{-1}$.

Example. Let us take $r = 0.5$ and $N = 200$. Then by (14), (15) and (16), $\rho^2 = 0.856$. □

Although the lower bound for P_e has been exhibited here in a closed form, it is still difficult to calculate it by the recurrence formulas (17), (18) for large N.

It is possible [11] to change the recurrence equations (17) into an explicit form

$$\alpha_n = c_1 x_1^n + c_2 x_2^n \tag{19}$$

Table 1. The resulting ρ^2 by (23) for $d = 1.01$ and different r and N

r	N			
	50	100	200	500
0.5	1	0.999	0.999	0.997
0.9	0.961	0.922	0.849	0.664
0.95	0.841	0.705	0.495	0.171
0.99	0.062	0.004	1.23×10^{-6}	4.82×10^{-13}

where x_1, x_2 are the roots of the quadratic equation

$$x^2 - (d + (d-2)r^2)x + ((d-1)r)^2 = 0 \tag{20}$$

and the coefficients are

$$c_1 = \frac{(d + (d-2)r^2) - x_2}{x_1 - x_2} \quad , \quad c_2 = 1 - c_1.$$

The explicit formula for the second recurrence relation (18) can be found in a similar manner. But unfortunately for large N, relations (19), (20) pose hard calculations.

For a "good" SG-system, we may expect $d \approx 1$, hence $((d-1)r)^2 << 1$, and then the following approximations for recurrence (17) result:

$$\forall n = 2, \ldots, N-1: \quad \alpha_n \approx (d + (d-2)r^2)\alpha_{n-1}$$

$$a_N \approx d\alpha_{N-1}$$

These produce the explicit formula

$$a_N = d(d + (d-2)r^2)^{N-1}. \tag{21}$$

In a similar manner, the following relation is obtained instead of the recurrence formula in (18):

$$b_N = d_1(d_1 + (d_1 - 2)r^2)^{N-1}. \tag{22}$$

Substituting (15), (21) and (22) into (14) we get finally

$$\rho^2 \approx \left(\frac{\sqrt{(1 - r^2)(1 + (1 - 2d^{-1})r^2)}}{(1 + (1 - 2t)r^2)} \right)^{N-1} \tag{23}$$

In Table 1 we present the calculated values of ρ^2 by (23) for different r and N, with $d = 1.01$.

There, one can see that for the chosen parameter $d = \left(1 - \frac{D}{2\sigma_S^2}\right)^{-2} \approx 1.01$ the SGS with embedding process by (12) is sufficiently secure if the samples of covertext have a small correlation ($r \leq 0.9$) but for large sample correlation (and this fact has been confirmed by exact calculation with recurrence formulas (17), (18)) the SGS is insecure. It is worth to note here that we may reduce an intersample correlation by a diversity of samples subjected to the embedding procedure.

Let us prove the formula for the error probability P_e for a legal user of the SG-system, i.e. an user knowing the secret sequence W^N, under the condition of additive noise attack and informed decoder. The embedding procedure by (12) can be specified as follows

$$X^{N_0} = aS^{N_0} + (-1)^b W^{N_0}$$

where $N_0 \leq N$ is the block length to embed one information bit $b \in \{0, 1\}$.

After the attack by additive zero-mean noise Z^{N_0} with variance σ_Z^2 we get

$$\tilde{X}^{N_0} = X^{N_0} + Z^{N_0}$$

The correlation informed receiver of the legal user should take its decision about the information bit $\tilde{b}$ by the following rule:

$$\Lambda = \sum_{n=1}^{N_0} \left(\tilde{X}(n) - aS(n) \right) W(n) \quad \Rightarrow \quad \tilde{b} = \begin{cases} 0 & \text{if } \Lambda \geq 0 \\ 1 & \text{if } \Lambda < 0 \end{cases}$$

where $\left(\tilde{X}(n) \right)_{n \leq N_0}$, $(S(n))_{n \leq N_0}$, $(W(n))_{n \leq N_0}$ are samples of $\tilde{X}^{N_0}$, S^{N_0}, W^{N_0} respectively. Then due to the Central Limit Theorem of Probability Theory, the probability of a bit error P, for any probability distribution of Z^{N_0}, can be expressed [12] as:

$$P \approx Q \left(\sqrt{N_0 \frac{D \left(1 - \frac{D}{4\sigma_S^2} \right)}{\sigma_Z^2}} \right) \tag{24}$$

where $Q : x \mapsto \frac{1}{\sqrt{2\pi}} \int_x^{+\infty} e^{-\frac{t^2}{2}} dt$.

Let us define the *distortion of covertext after attack* as

$$\text{var} \left(\tilde{X}^{N_0} - S^{N_0} \right) = D + \sigma_Z^2$$

and *signal-to-noise ratios* just *after embedding* η_w and *after attack* η_a, as:

$$\eta_w = \frac{\sigma_S^2}{D} \quad , \quad \eta_a = \frac{\sigma_S^2}{D + \sigma_Z^2}.$$

Now, using (24) the bit error probability P can easily be expressed in terms of η_w and η_a as

$$P \approx Q \left(\sqrt{N_0 \frac{(4\eta_w - 1)\, \eta_a}{4 \left(\eta_w - \eta_a \right) \eta_w}} \right) \tag{25}$$

If $\eta_w \gg 1$, this probability can be approximated as $P \approx Q \left(\sqrt{\frac{N_0}{\eta - 1}} \right)$ where $\eta = \frac{\eta_w}{\eta_a}$.

We may express now the parameter d presented in (23) in terms of η_w as

$$d = \left(1 - \frac{D}{2\sigma_S^2} \right)^{-2} = \left(1 - \frac{1}{2\eta_w} \right)^{-2} = \frac{4\eta_w^2}{(2\eta_w - 1)^2} \tag{26}$$

Example. Let us take $\eta_w = 100$, $\eta_a = 70$ and $N = 500$. Then we get by (26) that $d = 1.01$ and $t = 0.995$. The calculation by (23) for $r = 0.9$ gives $\rho^2 = 0.664$. On the other hand we have, by (25), that $P \approx Q(\sqrt{11.6}) \approx 3 \times 10^{-4}$ for $N_0 = 5$. This means that we are able to embed 100 bits of information in a secure manner (because ρ^2 is close to 1) and simultaneously to get enough reliability of these bits extraction by the legal user. $\qquad\qquad\square$

For a blind decoder, the decision about the information bit $\hat{b}$ is taken as

$$\tilde{\Lambda} = \sum_{n=1}^{N_0} \tilde{X}(n) W(n) \;\Rightarrow\; \hat{b} = \begin{cases} 0 & \text{if } \tilde{\Lambda} \geq 0 \\ 1 & \text{if } \tilde{\Lambda} < 0 \end{cases}$$

It can be proved [13] that the error probability for blind decoder can be approximated as

$$\tilde{P} \approx Q\left(\sqrt{N_0 \frac{(4\eta_w - 1)\,\eta_a}{4\,(\eta_w - \eta_a + \eta_w \eta_a)\,\eta_w}} \right) \tag{27}$$

If $\eta_w \gg 1$ we get from (27), $\tilde{P} \approx Q\left(\sqrt{\frac{N_0}{\eta_w}} \right)$.

Example. Under the same conditions as in previous example, we get the probability $\tilde{P} \approx 1.2 \times 10^{-2}$ if only $N_0 = 500$. This means that one bit can be embedded in an "almost secure" manner (since ρ^2 is close to 1). $\qquad\qquad\square$

In order to increase the number of bits embedded into a covertext for the case of a blind decoder, it is necessary to use the so called *informed encoder* as, for instance, improved spread spectrum technique (ISS) [14] or quantized projection technique (QP) [15]. However both of these techniques should be revised in terms of steganography. We are going to consider this problem in the near future.

4   Conclusion

In this paper, a novel criterion of undetectability of SGS based on Bhattacharyya distance has been proposed. We state that for some models of SGS, this notion is more convenient for calculations and analysis than the commonly used relative entropy criterion. In fact, the new criterion is based on a symmetric measure and gives both lower and upper bounds for the Bayesian probability error for optimal hypothesis testing. We show an application of this criterion to performance evaluation for optimal detecting of the SGS with Gaussian exponential correlated covertext and additive white noise watermark.

The last model of covertext embedding is of, both theoretical and practical, interest to steganography. In fact, we cannot provide perfectly undetectable SGS in practice because it is not known exactly the probability distribution of the covertext. What we have to do is just the design of an almost undetectable SGS, which is robust to covertext distributions. Since stegotext as a rule may include device noises [5] that can be approximated by colored Gaussian noise, the problem of SGS detecting consists in the discrimination of two Gaussian processes. Although the correlation matrix of a device noise is not necessary exponential, we may assume that formula (23) differs not so much from the real situation whenever the correlation of the adjacent sample in the covertext is not too large (say, at most 0.9) and the distortion due to embedding is small. In these conditions, we are able to design a real SGS with scaled stegotext and additive white noise watermark that is both secure and reliable, at least against additive noise attack.

Of course the assumption about informed decoder is too restrictive in practice whereas the use of blind decoders results in very lower data transmission rate. Therefore there is an open problem consisting on how to adapt informed encoder (as ISS or QP) into SG-systems.

References

1. Cachin, C.: An information-theoretic model for steganography. In: Aucsmith, D. (ed.) IH 1998. LNCS, vol. 1525, pp. 306–318. Springer, Heidelberg (1998)
2. Cover, T.M., Thomas, J.A.: Elements of Information Theory. John Wiley, Chichester (1991)
3. Poor, H.V.: An Introduction to Signal Detection and Estimation. Springer, Heidelberg (1994)
4. Wang, Y., Moulin, P.: Steganalysis of block-structured stegotext. In: Security, Steganography, and Watermarking of Multimedia Contents. SPIE Proceedings, vol. 5306, San Jose, California USA, pp. 477–488 (2004)
5. Sallee, P.: Model-based steganography. In: Kalker, T., Cox, I., Ro, Y.M. (eds.) IWDW 2003. LNCS, vol. 2939, pp. 154–167. Springer, Heidelberg (2004)
6. Kailath, T.: The divergence and Bhattacharyya distance measures in signal selection. IEEE Trans. Commun. Tech. 15, 52–60 (1967)
7. Korzhik, V.I., Fink, L.M.: Error-correcting Codes on Channels with Random Structure (in Russian), Svyaz, Moscow (1975)
8. Van Trees, H.L.: Detection, Estimation, and Modulation Theory. Parts I-II. John Wiley, Chichester (1973)
9. Huang, J., Mumford, D.: Statistics of natural images and models. In: Proc. IEEE Conf. Computer Vision and Pattern Recognition, pp. 541–547 (1999)
10. Horn, R.A., Johnson, C.R.: Matrix Analysis. Cambridge University Press, Cambridge (1983)
11. Hall, M.: Combinatorial Theory. John Wiley & Sons, Chichester (1986)
12. Korzhik, V., Lee, M.H., Morales-Luna, G.: Stegosystems based on noisy channels. In: IX Reunión Española de Criptología y Seguridad de la Información, Universidad Autónoma de Barcelona (2006)
13. Korzhik, V., Morales-Luna, G., Lee, M.H.: On the existence of perfect stegosystems. In: Barni, M., Cox, I., Kalker, T., Kim, H.J. (eds.) IWDW 2005. LNCS, vol. 3710, pp. 30–38. Springer, Heidelberg (2005)
14. Malvar, H.S., Florêncio, D.: Improved spread spectrum: A new modulation technique for robust watermarking. IEEE Trans. on Signal Processing 51, 898–905 (2001)
15. Pérez-Freire, L., Comesaña-Alfaro, P., Pérez-González, F.: Detection in quantization-based watermarking: performance and security issues. In: P.W. Wong, E.J. Delp (eds). Security, Steganography, and Watermarking of Multimedia Contents. SPIE Proceedings, vol. 5681, San Jose, California USA, pp. 721–733 (2005)

Secure Steganography Using Gabor Filter and Neural Networks

Mansour Jamzad and Zahra Zahedi Kermani*

Department of Computer Engineering,
Sharif University of Technology, Tehran, Iran
jamzad@sharif.edu, zahedike@ce.sharif.edu

Abstract. The main concern of steganography (image hiding) methods is to embed a secret image into a host image in such a way that it causes minimum distortion to the host; to make it possible to extract a version of secret image from the host in such a way that the extracted version of secret image be as similar as possible to its original version (this should be possible even after usual attacks on the host image), and to provide ways of embedding secret images with larger size into a given host image. In this paper we propose a method that covers all above mentioned concerns by suggesting the idea of finding from an image data base, the most suitable host for a given secret image. In our method, the secret and host images are divided into blocks of size 4×4. Each block in secret image is taken as a texture pattern for which using Gabor filter, the most similar block is found among the blocks of host image candidates. Using this similarity criterion and Kohonen neural network, the most suitable host image is selected from an image database. Embedding is done by placing the blocks of secret image on their corresponding blocks in the selected host image. The location addresses of blocks in host that were replaced by blocks of secret image are saved. They are converted to a bit string that is embedded in DCT coefficients of the hybrid image. Our experimental results showed a high level of capacity, robustness and minimum distortion when using standard images as secret and host images.

Keywords: Steganography, Gabor Filter, Texture similarity, Kohonen Neural Networks, DCT, Image database.

1 Introduction

Recent progresses in digital communication has made it possible to use intelligent methods for secret communication. One such method is image hiding in which a secret image is hidden in a host or cover image. The modified host image that contains the secret image is referred to as hybrid (stego) image.

There are several methods for hiding a secret image in a host image. Mainly they can be divided into methods that embed the secret image into the host

---

* Miss Z.Zahedi Kermani obtained her MS in computer engineering in 2001 and parts of this work was accomplished during her graduate studies.

Y.Q. Shi (Ed.): Transactions on DHMS III, LNCS 4920, pp. 33–49, 2008.

image in spatial domain and those that use transform domain. For spatial domain methods, the simplest methods are those that modify the least significant bits of pixels in the host image [1,2]. The advantages of these methods are their simplicity but they are weak in resisting simple attacks such as compression, etc. In these methods the capacity of embedding a secret image is limited and an increase in capacity severely influences the visual quality of hybrid image.

Image hiding techniques that are implemented in transform domain have made it possible to take advantage of features in human visual system [3,4]. These methods are more robust with respect to compression and some transforms, because they focus on the same features of image as compression techniques do. As another example, we can refer to [5] that uses the middle frequency coefficients of DCT and the quantization table of JPEG to embed a secret image. Also in [6] the authors have used the embedded zero tree Wavelet (EZW) to encode a host image to embed a secret image. In [7] Wavelet transform is applied both on cover and secret image to produce their SPIHT (set partitioning in hierarchical trees) encoded version. Then the encoded cover image is used as the carrier for the encoded secret image.

The spread spectrum techniques that are implemented in frequency domain, can provide high robustness regarding usual attacks. This is due to the fact that they consider the hidden message as a narrow-band signal and spread it over a wider frequency band. One disadvantage of these methods is that, since they have to merge the key into a noisy pattern and then embed the merged data into the frequency domain coefficients, this process may cause severe degradation in host image depending on the noisy pattern [8].

All these methods try to embed a given secret image into one particular cover image. The capacity and visual perception quality of final hybrid image highly depends on the size and content of both the secret and cover images. In fact, increasing the size of secret image not only will reduce the quality of hybrid image but also will reduce its robustness with respect to general attacks.

According to our survey on present methods, it seems that the main problem is their low capacity, because they do not have a preprocessing step to select the best suitable cover image for a given secret image. As a result, the capacity and visual perception of the hybrid image is limited depending on the size and content of secret image and the give host image. In addition they do not use the error control codes for improving the robustness of key.

Generally, capacity, visual perception and resistance are three criteria that are used to compare the performance of image hiding methods. Figure 1 shows the relation between these three criteria. For example,if the first criterion is assumed constant, and the second one is increased, then the third criterion decreases subsequently. Depending on the size and content of both secret and host images, the appropriate level of each criteria will be determined.

Most image hiding method try to remain loyal to the assumption that the host image is fixed, and by the time that the secret image becomes available, they will embed it into that particular host. Although in practice the above assumption might be a fact in some situations, but we can think of many other applications,

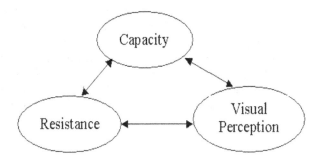

Fig. 1. Relation between three criterion: capacity, visual perception and resistance

where the aim is to have a secure method for embedding a secret image in any host, as long as the main concerns in image hiding is satisfied.

Therefore, in this paper we proposed a method that assumes the freedom of selecting the host for a given secret image, because in image hiding, the host image acts as a carrier and its content is not important to us. In our method for a given secret image, the most suitable host is selected from an image database in such a way that it provides a balance level between capacity, visual perception and resistance (robustness).

In addition we introduced an error control code to improve the robustness of a location address bit string used to retrieve the secret image from the hybrid image.

We assume that the secret image is considered as a mosaic (blocks) of different textures [9]. If these blocks are placed over their similar blocks in host image in a known order, then by having the location address of these blocks and their placement order in host image, retrieving the secret image will be like solving a puzzle of disordered pieces when one has the key that provides the order of putting parts together. Figure 2 shows a visual presentation of this idea.

Our method assumes that the secret and cover images are of monochrome type. However, this method can be extend to color images as well. In this case,

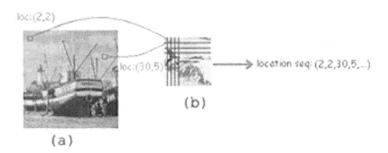

Fig. 2. a) Host image, (b) Secret image. The 1st and 2nd block of secret image are replaced in location (2,2) and (30,5) of the host image, respectively.

we can convert both the secret and cover images using YC_bC_r color model and perform our method on the Y channel (e.g. monochrome version of the color image).

The rest of this paper is organized as follows: In section 2 different steps of our algorithm is described. In section 3 we evaluate the performance of our method. In section 4 it is shown how the secret image can be extracted in case the hybrid image is lost. In section 5 we describe how the performance of our method can be improved by increasing the number of host images. And finally we give our conclusion on this research.

2   Our Algorithm

We describe how to find the best candidate host image from an image database in such a way that its content is most similar to that of a given secret image. Our image database contained 6 standard images of size 128×128, and the secret images were of size 64×64. The main idea of content based similarity is based on finding similar texture patterns (i.e. similar blocks of size 4×4) in secret and host image(s) and save their location addresses in host image(s) as a bit string. The reason for selecting block size of 4×4 is that it should be of a number as 2^n, to fit a fix number of times into times into host and secret images that are assumed to be of size 2^m, too. Some possible candidate values for n are $1, 2, 3 or 4$, that provides the block size of 2×2, 4×4, 8×8 or 16×16, respectively. Texture similarities on blocks of size 2×2 and 16×16 are not reliable because of too few and too many possible combination of gray level values within the block. The reason of selecting block size of 4×4 instead of 8×8 was because it is easier to find more perceptual similarities between textures of size 4×4. Therefore, replacing a block of size 4×4 in host with its most similar one from the secret image, produces less visible distortion to the host compared to block size of 8×8.

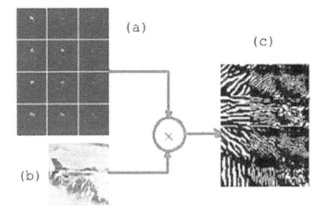

Fig. 3. Applying a bank of 12 Gabor filters with 4 angles and 3 scales on a secret image of size 64×64

As a similarity measure for textures we have used Gabor filter analysis provided in [9]. In this method the similarity is determined by comparison of a feature vector calculated for a block of size 4×4 in secret image and a set of feature vectors constructed for blocks of host images. The feature vector of host images of our image database are saved in a feature vector database. In the following sections we use the term block for a sub-image of size 4×4.

2.1 Selecting Appropriate Parameters for Gabor Filter

We have implemented a bank of Gabor filters using different scales and angles (i.e. parameters) [10]. Different values for these parameters can be selected, but it has been shown that using six angles can provide a complete representation of the image. In our implementation we found that using 4 angles (i.e. 0, 45, 90 and 135 degrees) and 3 scales (i.e. 1,2 and 3) provides acceptable performance in determining texture similarities. Four angles and three scales produce 12 Gabor filters that are applied on the secret image. Figure 3 shows the procedure of applying Gabor filter on a secret image. Each of 12 images in Fig.3(a) shows the real value of Gabor filter that is mapped in the gray scale range of $[0 - 255]$ for visualization purpose. Fig 3(b) is the secret image and the tile images on Fig 3(c) are the results of convolving the corresponding Gabor filters with a secret image.

The procedure shown in Fig 3 is applied on all candidate host images in our image database as well. In this way, as shown in Fig 3(c) for each candidate host image, we obtain a set of 12 images that are the result of convolving Gabor filters with that host image.

2.2 Creating a Database for Feature Vectors

Comparison of texture similarity between secret and host images is based on feature vector comparison. The secret and host images are divided into blocks. For each block, the mean and standard deviation of its corresponding blocks in each of 12 filtered images of Fig 3(c) is calculated. In this way, a 24 component feature vector is obtained. Fig 4 shows a visualization of this procedure.

Within this procedure, we have calculated the above mentioned feature vector for all host images in our image database and created a feature vector database. Assuming to have N images of size 256×256 in the image database, the number of entries for feature vector database will be equal to $N \times ((256 \times 256)/(4 \times 4)) = N \times 4096$.

2.3 Using Kohonen Neural Network as a Mean of Fast Search

Due to the large number of records in feature vector database, we must have an efficient method for indexing and searching in it. Therefore, the input records of this database were fed into a Kohonen neural network (NN) that is a self organizing neural network. At the beginning, there was no particular structure among the records in this database, but after training, the texture patterns in all host images were grouped in a cluster. The training algorithm uses a mechanism called "selecting the winning node". In this mechanism, for each input

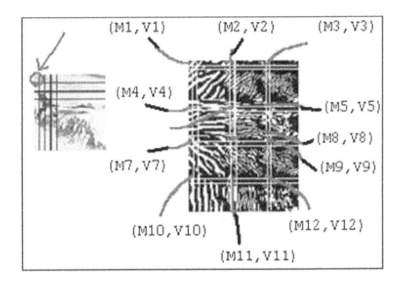

Fig. 4. Visualization of the procedure that calculates a 24 component feature vector. The component vector is defined as (m1,m2,...m12,v1,v2,...v12).

feature vector, the Euclidean distance between it and all nodes is calculated. The node with minimum distance is selected to be the winning node (e.g. this is the matching procedure of an input feature vector with a cluster of feature vectors in Kohonen NN [11]. Then the weight of this winning node and its neighbors are updated. By implementing this algorithm on all feature vectors in database, the feature vectors will be grouped in such a way that those close to each other will always activate the same node. The initial learning rate of this network was 1, and the feature vector records were given to the network for training purpose, eight times, where the learning rate was reduced in half each time.

2.4   How to Find the Best Host Image for Embedding

We have used the above mentioned feature vectors to find the most similar texture in image database. For each block in secret image, its feature vector is calculated and is given to the neural network. At network's output, only one node is activated. This node indicates the index of a group of similar blocks in the image database. In this group, by using the feature vector distance measure, the nearest block of an image in database to the block of secret image is determined.

This procedure is carried on for all blocks of the secret image. At the end, the image in database having the most number of similar blocks, is chosen to be the host image. Figure 5 shows an illustration of this procedure that shows the Boat image was the most suitable to host the Jet secret image.

Although the quality of the stego-image (hybrid image) highly depends on the host image selected from the database, but since this selection is done based on a similarity measure, therefore, the quality of stego-image depends on the number

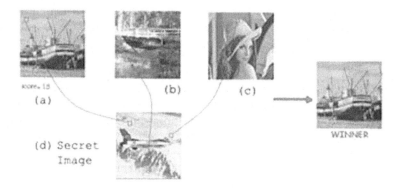

Fig. 5. Illustration of the procedure for selecting the most suitable host image for a given secret image

of images and their variety made available in image database. In practice, the users of such systems can carefully provide a class or family of images in database such that it could give a high level of similarity to a given class of secrete images.

However, if we add M images (each having K, 4×4 blocks) to our existing database, then the training time of NN will increase linearly with a factor of $M \times K$. However, since training is done only once, this increase of time can be acceptable.

To evaluate the increase of time in searching for the most similar image in the database, we refer to the process of selecting the most similar image as described in above. In this process, for each block of secret image, only one node in NN is activated. Therefore this part does not require any additional time. However, each activated node in NN refers to a list of images in which a block most similar to the examining block of the secret image was found. It is clear that if the number of images in database increases, this list will be longer (more number of images will appear in this list). When the above procedure is carried on for all K blocks of secret image, we will have K lists, each containing image names that contain blocks most similar to a corresponding block of the secrete image.

If the number of images in database is increased, the number of elements in these lists will increase linearly. The final step of fining the most similar image from database, is to go through all these lists and find the image with maximum number of repetition (e.g. the image with most number of similar blocks to the blocks of secret image). As a result, at this step, we will expect to have a linear increase in search time in these lists.

2.5   How to Hide and Retrieve the Secret Image

After choosing the host image, for each block in secret image, the most similar block to it in host image is found and is replaced with that block of secret image. The position (location address) of this block in host image is saved. This procedure is repeated for all blocks in the secret image. At the end of this procedure, we have a modified host image in which the entire secret image is embedded. At this stage, the sequence of above mentioned location addresses is saved into a location bit string. The image obtained in this step is called first step hybrid image. The rest of hiding procedure is summarized as follows:

1. Apply DCT with block size of 8×8 on the first step hybrid image.
2. Apply Hamming code to the location address bit string. The reason for using the Hamming code is due to its ability to recover the error bits in the extracted location address bit string. This procedure will improve the security of extracting the secret image from the stego-image, in case of degradation imposed on it.
3. Choose a seed for a random number (key) and construct a sequence of location addresses. These addresses indicate the position of elements (8×8 blocks) of DCT in first step hybrid image, in which bits of secured location bit string (e.g. as described in step 2) will be embedded.
4. Modify middle frequencies of DCT coefficients in randomly selected blocks to embed bits of location address bit string. The reason for selecting middle frequencies is that these frequencies are less likely to be modified by compression methods. The number of DCT coefficients in the middle frequencies need to be changed depends on the number of bits needed to represent the secured location address.
5. Apply inverse DCT transform to obtain the modified host image (final hybrid image) which contains the secret image.

In retrieval stage, in order to extract the secret image, we apply DCT on final hybrid image. Then using the same key, we find the addresses of all blocks which DCT coefficients were modified to embed the location address bit string. In this way, the bit string that contains the location addresses is retrieved. Thus, those blocks in host image that contain the blocks of secret image, are determined. As a result the entire secret image is extracted.

3   Performance Evaluation of Our Method

Our algorithm was implemented using Visual C++ on a PC with Pentium II processor of 500 MHz. The image database contained 65 images of fixed size 128×128. The secret image was of size 64×64. All images were 8 bit gray scale. For evaluation purpose, we used PSNR measure that is defined as follows:

$$PSNR = 10 \log_{10} \frac{L^2}{MSE} \tag{1}$$

$$MSE = \frac{1}{N} \sum_{i=1}^{N} (x_i - \bar{x}_i)^2 \tag{2}$$

In the above equations, L is the maximum gray level value, which is 255 for 8 bit gray scale image. x_i is the real value of the signal and $\bar{x}_i$ is the signal value after modification. N is the total number of signals.

The amount of error in extracted signal (i.e. bit string of location address) is measured by Bit Error Rate (BER) that is equal to the number of error bits in extracted signal divided by total number of bits in original location address bit string. In our evaluations, we considered the effect of BER on three features such as capacity, perceived quality and robustness of hybrid images, as described in following.

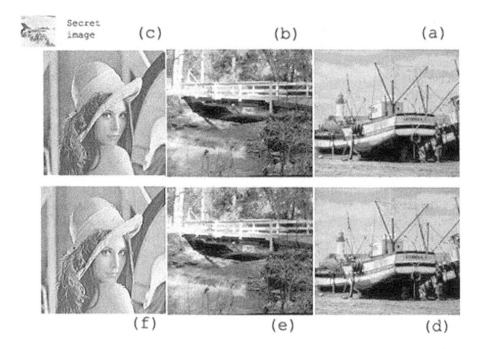

Fig. 6. An example of selecting three candidate images to host a secret image. The PSNR was 30, 28 and 29 for images in (a),(b) and (c), respectively. Images (e),(f) and (g) show the host image in which the secret image is hidden.

3.1   Performance of Selecting the Host Image

Selecting the appropriate host image highly depends on the variety of images available in image database. We shall note that there is no need to have a host image similar to the secret image or even there is no need to have similar objects in host and secret images. Figure 6 shows the performance of our algorithm by selecting different host images. According to PSNR, Fig 6 (a), (c) and (b) are the 1st, 2nd and 3rd candidates for the given secret image, respectively. Figures (d),(e) and (f) show the host images in which the same secret image is hidden.

In fact, MSE increases for candidate host images that have lower similarity with the secret image while PSNR decreases in such cases.

3.2 Performance with Respect to Capacity and Comparison with Related Works

The capacity of data hiding increases proportional to the increase in the variety of textures available in host image. Such host images give higher PSNR ratio compared to images having less variety in textures.

As described in section 2.5, in our method the location address bit string that is saved in middle frequencies of DCT coefficients of blocks of size 8×8 of final hybrid image. This bit string represents the location addresses of blocks in host image that are replaced by their corresponding most similar blocks of secret image.

There are some other methods of data hiding [13,14] that take the secret data as a binary data (for example for an eight bit per pixel secret image of size 64×64 it uses $64 \times 64 \times 8 = 32768$ bits) and replace them in middle frequencies of DCT coefficients of blocks of size 8×8 of original host image. Then the final hybrid image is obtained by applying inverse DCT. These methods do not use any similarity measure between blocks of host and secret image.

We have compared the performance of our method (named MY DCT) with that of above mentioned ones (named OLD DCT) by comparing the PSNR of the original image and the final hybrid image in each method. This result is shown in figure 7. As it is seen, in both methods the PSNR decreases with respect to increase in capacity (number of bits embedded) while our algorithm could provide better PSNR in all cases. In addition, in both methods the image quality decreases while the number of bits in secret image increases.

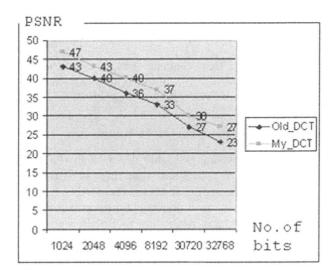

Fig. 7. The relation between PSNR and the number of bits embedded in host image. Old DCT indicates using direct embedding of bits in DCT coefficients and My-DCT shows embedding using Gabor filter.

3.3   The Effect of Error Bit

Any error in the extracted location address bit string that represents block location addresses in host image, is equivalent to losing the data of one or more blocks in secret image. It means that choosing an appropriate method for embedding the location address bit string in DCT coefficients is of high importance. Therefore, we applied error control coding methods to increase the performance of correct extraction of location address bit string. We have used Hamming code to protect this bit string. However, one might use different methods for error control coding that gives higher protection by the cost of increase in overhead bits. This topic is widely addressed in cryptography and related topics.

3.4   Robustness

One of the weak points in most image hiding algorithms is that if the host image goes under some attacks, then extracting secret image without applying pre-processing routines such as error control codes becomes very difficult. We have tested our method against JPEG compression attack with quality factor of Q=75, 50, 25, 10 and 5. (e.g. Q factor ranges from 1 to 100, a factor of 1 produces the smallest, worst quality image and a factor of 100 produces the largest, best quality image). In all compressed images with above mentioned quality factors still we were able to extract the secret image but with lower quality, depending

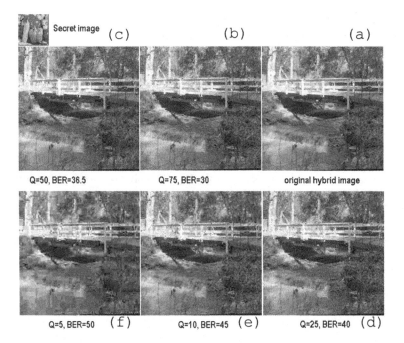

Fig. 8. The effect of compression on robustness of our method. In all images the secret image could be extracted from the hybrid image.

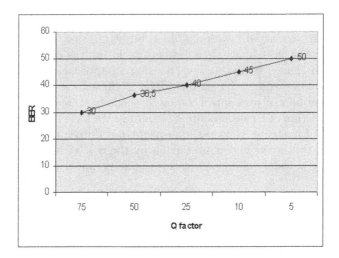

Fig. 9. he effect of compression on robustness, by means of the relation between quality factor in JPEG and BER (Bit Error Rate) when the Peppers and Bridge images were selected as secret and host images, respectively

on the value of Q. However, this low quality can be improved by post-processing image restoration or enhancement methods.

An example is shown in figure 8 the Peppers and Bridge images were selected as secret and host images, respectively. The bit error rate (BER) shown under each image changed from 30, 36.5, 40, 45 and 50, for images (b-f), respectively. BER increases with decrease in Q factor. Figure 8(a) is the Bridge image in which the secret image is hidden without compression. Figure 9 shows the relation between BER and Q Factor.

3.5   Performance Evaluation with Respect to Stegoanalysis Methods

Stegoanalysis methods evaluate the robustness of stego image if it goes under a test to verify containing a secret image in it. In this section, we evaluate the security of the proposed algorithm using a blind steganalyzer. Universal steganalysers are composed of two important components [19]. These are feature extraction and feature classification. In feature extraction, a set of distinguishing statistics are obtained from a data set of images. There is no well-defined approach to obtaining these statistics, but often they are proposed by observing general image features that exhibit strong variation under embedding. Feature classification, operates in two modes. First, the obtained distinguishing statistics from both cover and stego images are used to train a classifier. Second, the trained classifier is used to classify an input image as either being cover image or carrying a hidden message (e.g. a stego image in our application).

One of the steganalysis techniques is wavelet-based steganalysis. This approach is proposed by Lyu and Farid [16,17] for feature extraction from images.

The authors argue that most of the specific steganalysis techniques concentrate on first order statistics, (i.e., histogram of DCT coefficients) since simple counter-measures could keep the first-order statistics intact, thus making the steganalysis technique useless. So they proposed building a model for natural images by using higher order statistics and then showed that images with messages embedded in them deviate from this model. Quadratic mirror filters are used to decompose the image into wavelet domain, after which statistics such as mean, variance, skewness, and kurtosis are calculated for each sub-band. Additionally the same statistics are calculated for the error obtained from a linear predictor of coefficient magnitudes of each sub-band, as the second part of the feature set. More recently, in [18], Lyu and Farid expanded their feature set to include a set of phase statistics. As noted in their work, these additional features have little effect on the performance of the steganalyzer.

We have tested our proposed method with a blind steganalyzer that uses only the original set of features as suggested in [17]. In this test, we selected 110 JPEG images from Washington Image Database [20] which included some popular images usually used in image processing algorithms. We resized these images into two sets of 110 images of size 256×256 and 512×512. These two sets were used as our cover image database.

In addition 65 images from the above mentioned 110 images were selected at random and resized into 64×64 as secret images.

For a given secret image, the best cover image is selected from the above mentioned cover image database and then using our proposed algorithm, the secret image is hidden in it. Since we have 65 secret images, the procedure of secret image embedding is repeated 65 times. At the end of this stage we have 65 steg-images.

We selected 40 of these steg-images at random. Also we picked up the clean version (i.e. the version before embedding the secret image) of the same 40 images.

Using wavelet based stegoanalyzer [17] we trained a Fisher Discriminant classifier for each set of 40 steg-images and clean images. We used this classifier to classify the remaining 25 steg and 25 clean images (e.g. from the set of 65 images described above). The results are reported with True positives and False positives measures, if they are determined to contain a secret image or be clean, respectively. The steps of randomly selecting 40 steg-images, etc, and then

Table 1. Wavelet-based steganalyzer detection accuracy obtained for secret images of size 64×64 and cover images of size 256×256 and 512×512, given in rows 1 and 2, respectively

Average Secret Image Size (KBytes)	Average Cover Image Size (KBytes)	Embedding Rate (Hidden data per bit)	False Positives Recognition	True Positives Recognition
4.3	63.5	0.067	32.28%	56%
4.3	256	0.016	32.57%	52.37%

classifying the remaining steg and clean images were repeated 8 times. The average detection accuracy are shown in columns 4 and 5 of Table 1.

The analysis of the method and the experimental results show that applying the wavelet based steganalysis method on clean and steg-images, can not reliably detect steg and non-steg images. Note that the performance of our method improves when the size of host image is increased from 256×256 to 512×512 for the same secret image of size 64×64.

4   Extracting Secret Image When the Final Hybrid Image Is Lost

One of the advantages of our method or any other method that selects the host according to its similarity to the secret image, is that even if the final hybrid image is not available (lost), still we can extract a low quality version of the secret image (e,g. pseudo-secret image). Because the original host is is known to us and is available in database and also we have the key, we can extract the correct order of 4x4 blocks representing the secret image from the original host. Theoretically, in this situation, the amount of similarity between the pseudo-secret image and the real secrete image depends on how well (similar) the host was selected. In addition the accuracy of similarity of host and secret images, highly depends on the number of images in database and how well those images were selected to become a good candidate for a wide range of secrete images. For example, for certain applications, we can add a family of well suited images in database in such a way that it provides the most similarity to a given family of secret images. However, since there is a high similarity between the extracted blocks from the original host and those blocks of original secret image, therefore, the obtained pseudo-secret image would have an acceptable similarity to the original secret image [12].

In addition, if the final hybrid image is degraded severely, we can assume the hybrid image in not available. Then, since we know the key and the original host image, therefore we extract a rough version of the secret image from the original host image as described in above.

On the other hand, since mostly, there are blocks in secret image that are similar to each other in texture content, therefore, we can use one block in host image (that is most similar to those in secret image) to represent all of those similar blocks in secret image. Using this similarity criterion, the capacity increases tremendously, but of course it will affect on the perceptual quality of the final extracted secret image, depending on the similarity measures used to select similar blocks in secret image.

5   Improving Performance by Selecting More Than One Host Image

Our experimental results showed that the overall performance of our method can be improved by selecting more than one host image to embed the secret

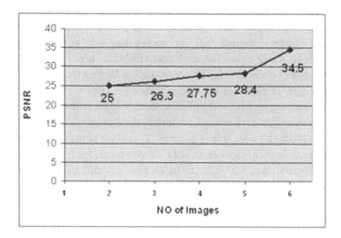

Fig. 10. The relation between PSNR and the number of host images used

image. That is, the blocks of secret image is distributed in two or more host images depending on the similarity measure being imposed. Figure 10 shows the performance of our method by comparing the PSNR while the number of host images increased from 2 to 6. The PSNR increased from 24 when using 2 host images to 34.5 in case of using 6 host images.

However, for a fixed size of secret image, if we use more than one host image, it will reduce the capacity of each host, that is it will host fewer number of blocks from the secret image. As a result due to fewer modifications in hosts, they will have less degradation compared with when using only one host. On the contrary, if we use more than one host, we can increase the size of secret image.

6   Conclusion

Performance of image hiding methods highly depends on the capacity and robustness of hybrid image and the similarity of retrieved secret image to its original version. All these should be achieved by minimum distortion to the host image. Most existing methods are based on the fact that a given secret image should be embedded into one particular host image. These methods provide certain amount of limitations in capacity, robustness and also similarity, because the host is not selected according to the content of the secret image and for some reasons it is selected to be the host.

These methods provide certain level of limitations in fulfilling the general concerns of steganography. However, if we assume that there are applications where there is no restriction on selecting the host image, then some new ideas in image hiding algorithms can explore. In this paper we suggested one such algorithm that we believe it provides a high level of capacity, robustness and also similarity, while maintaining the minimum distortion in the host image(s). Our main idea is based on dividing the secret image into small blocks of size 4×4

and consider these blocks as texture patterns. Then using the similarity measure provided by Gabor filter, for any given block in a secret image, the most similar block in a host image is found and the secret block is placed there. However, in order to achieve more capacity and also decrease host image distortion, we introduced the idea of embedding the secret image blocks into more than one host image. Therefore, if we develop an image database containing enough variety of images, then we can expect to find suitable image(s) to embed the desired secrete image in such a way that the requirements of capacity, robustness and visual perception are satisfied in an optimal level. Our experimental results confirmed that using multiple host images, not only allows us to increase the size of secret image to any desired size, but also reduces the amount of distortions imposed on host images.

We believe that our method can produce even better results, if we use several image databases developed for different image classes (i.e. flowers, faces, cars, foods, nature, etc.) and use the right database for a given secrete image. The idea of using different class of image databases are widely used in content based image retrieval.

In this regard another approach is to use at least three databases for images with low, medium and high details. Then we can select the database according to the level of detail in the given secret image. There are many known methods for finding the level of detail in an image [15]. In our future work, we are going to implement this idea and evaluate its performance.

Moreover, we believe, allowing the option of selecting the most suitable host for a given secret image, could lead to many new methods in steganography.

Acknowledgments

We would like to highly appreciate the efforts of Miss H.Sajedi who is currently doing her PhD in Department of Computer Engineering, Sharif University of Technology, for preparing the stegoanalysis tests for our method.

References

1. Tsai, P., Hu, Y.C., Chang, C.C.: An image hiding technique using block truncation coding. In: Proceedings of Pasific Rim Workshop on Digital Steganography, July 2002, Kitakyushu, Japan, pp. 54–64 (2002)
2. Wang, R.Z., Lin, J.F., Lin, J.C.: Image hiding by optimal LSB substitution and genetic algorithm. Journal of Pattern Recognition 34(3), 671–683 (2001)
3. Chae, J.J., Mukherjee, D., Manjunath, B.S.: Color Image Embedding using Multi-dimensional Lattice Structures. In: Proceeding of IEEE International Conference of Image Processing (ICIP 1998), October, 1998, Chicago, vol. 1, pp. 460–464 (1998)
4. Kim, Y.S.: A wavelet based watermarking method for digital images using human visual system. Sogang University (1999)
5. Chang, C.C., Chen, L.Z., Chung, L.Z.: A steganograhpic method based upon JPEG and quantization table modification. Information Society 141, 123–138 (2002)

6. Spaukling, J., Hoda, H., Shirazi, M.N., Kawaguchi, E.: BPCS steganography using EZW lossy compression images. Pattern Recognition Letters 23, 1579–1587 (2002)
7. Tsai, P., Hu, Y.C., Chang, C.C.: A progressive secret reveal system based on SPIHT image transmission. Journal of Signal Processing: Image Communication 19, 285–297 (2004)
8. Marvel, L.M.: Image steganography for hidden communication. University of Delaware, Spring (1999)
9. Ma, W.Y.: Texture features and learning similarity. University of California, Santa Barbara (1996)
10. Manjunath, B.S.: Gabor wavelet transform and application to problems in early vision. In: Proc.26th conference on signals, systems and computers, October 1992, Pacific Grove, CA, pp. 796–800 (1992)
11. Principe, J.C., Euliano, N.R., Lefebvre, W.C.: Neural and Adaptive Systems: Fundamentals Through Simulations. John Wiley and Sons, Chichester (2000)
12. Zahedi Kermani, Z., Jamzad, M.: A robust steganography algorithm based on texture similarity using Gabor filter. In: The 5th IEEE Int. Symposium Signal Processing and Information Technology (ISSPIT), December 18-21, 2005, Athens, Greece (2005)
13. Csurka, C., Deguillaume, F., Ruanaidh, J.J.K.O., Pun, T.: A Bayesian, approach to affine transformation resistant image and video watermarking. In: Proc. Int. Workshop on Information Hiding, September 1999, Dresden, Germany (1999)
14. Piva, A., Barni, M., Bartonili, F., Cappellini, V.: DCT-based watermark recovering without resorting to the un- uncorrupted original image. In: IEEE Int. Conference on Image Processing, October 1997, Santa Barbara, CA, vol. 1, pp. 520–523 (1997)
15. Franco, R., Malah, D.: Adaptive Image Partitioning for Fractal Coding Achieving Designated Rates Under a Complexity Constraint. In: IEEE 2001 International Conference on Image Processing (2001)
16. Lyu, S., Farid, H.: Detecting hidden messages using higher-order statistics and support vector machines. In: Proc. 5th Int. Workshop on Information Hiding (2002)
17. Lyu, S., Farid, H.: Steganalysis using color wavelet statistics and one-class support vector machines. In: Proc. SPIE 5306, pp. 35–45 (2004)
18. Lyu, S., Farid, H.: Steganalysis using higher order image statistics. IEEE Trans. Inf. Forens. Secur. 111–119 (2006)
19. Kharrazi, M., Husrev, T., Sencar, H.T., Memon, N.: 'Performance study of common image steganography and steganalysis techniques'. Journal of Electronic Imaging 15(4), 41–104 (2006)
20. http://www.cs.washington.edu/research/imagedatabase/groundtruth/

Oracle Channels

Ilaria Venturini

Laboratoire des Signaux et Systèmes (LSS)
École Supérieure d'Électricité (Supélec)
3, rue Joliot Curie
91192 Gif sur Yvette Cedex - France
ilaria.venturini@lss.supelec.fr

Abstract. The paper is structured into three main parts. In the first part, we focus on information leakage through new covert channels, we term *oracle channels*, which occur in case *oracle attacks* are performed on watermarked digital media or multimedia. In the second part, we show how to counteract oracle channels without resorting to protection tools that are quite demanding for communication networks. In the third part, we follow the information-theoretic approach to show that the countermeasures proposed in the second part do reduce the secret information leakage that flows through oracle channels, without sensibly compromising the detector reliability in case no oracle attack is performed.

Keywords: Covert channels, Covert communications, Information hiding, Information leakage, Oracle attacks, Secure watermarking, Subliminal channels.

1 Introduction

Digital media have been used to host authorized secret information. From the communication perspective, authorized secret information that is hidden in them gives rise to communication channels named *subliminal channels* [1]. A subliminal channel is a communication channel having the following characteristic properties:

i) there are both sender and receiver as authorized parties who agree to share any private key, knowledge of details concerning the communication network (protocols, transmission strategies, layers, etc) and algorithms to be exploited;

ii) a subliminal channel is foreseen by the scheme designer within a cover channel that was designed for other purposes.

iii) it does not violate the cover channel security;

iv) it should be easy to detect by the authorized receiver, while difficult to detect by any unauthorized receiver.

Examples of subliminal channels are digital watermark channels, i.e. channels where the watermark is transmitted. Watermarks are media embedded into host

Y.Q. Shi (Ed.): Transactions on DHMS III, LNCS 4920, pp. 50–69, 2008.

media for several different goals depending on the application of interest. In fact, watermarks may convey information such as media's origin, intended destination, owner, content integrity etc. and maintain some desired property such as *imperceptibility, blindness, robustness, fragility, semi-fragility, security,* varying with the intended application area.

For what concerns unauthorized secret information, we are aware that some form of unauthorized covert communication may occur by means of techniques that were never intended to be used to convey information. For instance, the noise made by a device, as well as the amount of power drawn by a device, can be utilized to transmit information. On the Internet, information is often segmented into packets in order to be transmitted. Since n packets can be ordered in $n!$ ways, by selecting a specific ordering, information can be transmitted without storing extra information. During a communication protocol, the sender can exploit the acknowledgment timing so as to convey covert information, if the receiving party can repeat observations [2,3]. A security protocol is a distributed algorithm containing a set of prescribed message exchanges between parties over an insecure network. Their security usually relies on encryption, so that they are computation or communication demanding.

All these forms of covert communication give rise to channels that are cases of *covert channels.* The first definition of covert channel appeared in [4]. A covert channel is a communication channel which exploits a cover channel and violates a security policy. Different types of covert channels proliferated in the meanwhile. Covert channels that are known so far share the following characteristic aspects.

i) There are cooperating malicious or selfish parties, specifically the covert sender who conveys information through a cover communication channel (that was devised for other purposes) and some designated covert receivers. There is a predetermined agreed-upon arrangement by the communicating parties including private key sharing, knowledge of details concerning the communication network (protocols, transmission strategies, layers, etc) and algorithms to be exploited.

ii) A covert channel is not foreseen by the designer of the utilized cover channel.

iii) The security of the used cover channel is violated by a covert channel.

iv) A covert channel is difficult to detect. In [5] a procedure for automatically detecting whether covert information has been embedded into JPEG images from the Internet and the performed experimental results to discover this eventuality, are described. Watching traffic through a network, by the administrator or by the so-called network radar algorithms, in order to detect suspicious activity, is a widely used technique for detecting whether a covert channel is going on (see for instance [6]). This is a more difficult task in an ad hoc wireless than in a wired network. In fact, it is difficult to distinguish unusual from usual traffic in an ad hoc wireless network which is without a centralized control and where there is communication channel sharing.

v) A covert channel needs neither high rate (therefore no high capacity) nor particularly low loss rate since it can reduce its rate significantly (therefore it needs no constant rate).

vi) Covert information can be either stored in suitable locations or transmitted by the transmission modality. So far, a great attention has been devoted to covert channels in multilevel information systems, wired computer networks and, in the last few years, also in ad hoc wireless networks. For instance, on the Internet, special parts of a TCP/IP packet header that are not used as locations for transmission or that are optional, have been used to covertly send supplementary information that can be easily reassembled by the receiving party with the use of the *stego-key* [7]. In [8], covert low rate information is sent by a technique the authors refer to as generation of *phantom packets*. Covert channels on an autonomous wireless ad hoc network, composed of mobile nodes, have been described which utilize special parts of a reactive routing protocol, where initiation of routes occur according to demand [9,10]. In [11], timing attacks on implementations of RSA, Diffie-Hellman and other systems are described, under the hypothesis that the attacker can make reasonably accurate timing measurements.

Moreover, there are cases of unauthorized secret information transmission where covert information is not intentionally transmitted by a malicious or selfish covert sender, rather it is leaked by an attacker alone. Information leakage, as secret information that is revealed to an unauthorized party without any malicious sender, may occur in several scenarios and may require different computational efforts. For instance, *inference channels*, that have received considerable attention in the literature on secure databases, are covert channels such that stored sensitive information can be leaked from stored non-sensitive information [12]. Leak free channels do not exist so far and it seems unlikely that non-trivial ones shall be developed, even if security protocols are used.

Here we focus on *oracle attacks*, that can be considered as particular information leakage attacks which leak the secret watermark, hidden into watermarked digital media or multimedia. The evaluated watermark is removed in copyright and copy protection applications. We claim that every algorithm which makes use of some secret information should face in its very formulation possible information leakage to an unauthorized party. Thus a secure channel designer should aim at maximizing security by minimizing (secret) information leakage. Our problem is how to cope with information leakage threats by the very definition of algorithms without resorting to protections that turn out to be quite demanding, i.e. requiring a relevant communication network cost. A *network cost* is not a well-defined notion including computational complexity and network technological practicalities such as communication overhead as interactive connections, key management, accessing to huge data bases. A low network cost is a priority for wireless ad hoc networks [13].

Here we show that, from the communication perspective, oracle attacks form a new class of covert channels we term *oracle channels*. This helps us to formulate methods for counteracting them. Moreover, the counteracting methods we propose aim to keep low the network cost.

The rest of this paper is organized as follows. In Section 2 known oracle attacks are briefly recalled. In Section 3, new covert channels are described, specifically the oracle channels. In Section 4, tools to counteract oracle channels are premised. Three counteracting methods are presented in Section 5. In Section 6, the trade-off between counteracting oracle channels and detection reliability is analyzed by means of information-theoretic notions. Section 7 concludes the paper.

2 Known Oracle Attacks

For surveys on watermarking security the reader is referred to [14,15,16,17,18]. Here we focus on watermark evaluation as performed by oracle attacks.

2.1 The Oracle Model

There are several kinds of oracles: deterministic or probabilistic devices with a more or less decision/computation power, the most powerful being the Turing oracle. Specifically, an oracle attack deals with an algorithmic oracle which is either a hardware or a software device, the detector, whose input is the query and whose output is a binary decision answer on the input. The oracle evaluates a given detection formula on every input under a predetermined threshold and gives always the same answer on the same input. Such an oracle may give a false answer under an acceptable decision threshold, following a binary Hypothesis Testing. It works by exploiting secret data that are not public because of the designer's decision. Therefore there is the problem of keeping such data secret. To gain knowledge about such secret data, the attacker works as described in the following attacker model.

2.2 The Attacker Model

1. The attacker is active.
2. The attacker is allowed to use a sealed black box watermark detector on a chosen medium of interest. We observe that a black box detector is a quite realistic assumption since most honest users want to easily obtain right and quick decision answers about their media rather than to implement algorithms.
3. The attacker has unlimited access to the detector.
4. The attacker has no knowledge of the secret key but still has a knowledge of the used algorithms that varies with the watermarking scheme. In many cases, the attacker knows the detection formula, in others knows only some properties the detection formula has to meet, i.e. the attacker knows a family of formulas. If the attacker knows absolutely nothing about the algorithms, then the attacker should proceed randomly and interactively with the oracle in order to perform an oracle attack. Of course, the successful convergence problem of such an inefficient attack should be settled.
5. The attacker could exploit also the statistical profiling of the media. Therefore, the well-known Kerckhoffs assumption, where there are only the involved algorithms to be known, cannot be assumed with its full meaning [19].
6. The attacker does not dispose of the unwatermarked medium.

The first well-known oracle attack is the *sensitivity analysis attack* described for symmetric schemes designed for copy protection [20,21]. The detection formula, known to the attacker, is of linear correlation type and the watermark is binary. The authors are aware that the attack is effective under more general assumptions. Some variations of it can be adapted so as to become threats for several data hiding methods. The watermark is private as well as the decision thresholds thr, Thr, with $thr < Thr$ and $[thr, Thr]$ as the uncertainty interval. The watermark is first evaluated by leakage in order to be removed. To this aim, a short path out of the detection region (geometrically represented), i.e. the region where the detection values are greater than the decision threshold, is exploited. Such a short path is the normal to (the tangent of) the detection region. Once such a direction has been determined, the considered medium is forced by the attacker to move along it by some amount, iteratively and interactively with the oracle, until the detection region boundary is crossed. The watermark is estimated as a zero mean binary vector. The complexity of the sensitivity attack is linear with the size L_x of the input. Its stochastic convergence has been proven in [22].

The *gradient descendent attack* is a version of the sensitivity attack where the watermark is estimated by using a gradient descendent algorithm.

In [22], a non-iterative formulation of the sensitivity analysis attack, at a copyright protection setting, obtains the watermark as the solution of a linear system with N equations and N unknowns, by at most $L_x + 1$ operations, starting from suitable guess values. The watermark is an arbitrary vector of real numbers. Such an attack is also extended to a wide family of detection functions including linear correlation, provided that the gradient of the detection function is calculated. Such a method shows that if the attacker knows the detection formula, established numerical methods for solving equation systems may be used to calculate the unknown watermark.

In [23], a formulation of the sensitivity analysis attack is given by exploiting the well known Newton iterative approximation method. Therefore the attacker needs only to know that the used (unknown) detection formula meets the Newton's method hypothesis, namely differentiability, and to start from a good guess value. Such a method shows that established numerical approximation methods may enlarge the class of detection formulas to all formulas that meet the assumptions of the used approximation method. Convergence, at least locally, is assured provided that the initial guess value is good enough.

In [24] an iterative sensitivity attack is formulated for quantization-based watermarking.

In [25,26] a sensitivity attack variation is outlined for *selective integrity* verification watermarking schemes. Although in the integrity scenario the attacker's aim is not unauthorized removal of the watermark, the watermark evaluation phase typical of oracle attacks remains crucial. The focus in those papers is on countermeasures: in [25] only a countermeasure that is based on time delay is discussed; in [26] also randomization is addressed. In the present paper, the setting is not limited to the integrity application.

3   A Channel Model for Oracle Attacks

Several communication channel models for watermarking have been formulated. We recall that watermarking communication has first received an oversimplified modeling where the watermark is the information and the cover signal is the channel that limits the detection of the watermark since the watermark is a weak signal. Then watermarking has been modeled as communication with side information at the embedding, being the host known at the embedding phase [15,27]. Later, watermarking communication has been modeled as a communication channel having a covert channel for transmitting the watermark, with side information available at the embedding as well as at the detection phases [28]. Such a covert channel is publicly known to exist and does not violate security. Therefore it is better classified as a subliminal channel.

A formulation following the theory of games has also been given, where the scheme designer wants to maximize the rate of reliable transmission whereas the attacker wants to minimize it [28,29].

Our approach is different here. We aim at modeling oracle attacks on actual environments as sketched in Figures 1, 2 and 3. Scenarios in Figures 2 and 3 require a major network cost than that in Figure 1.

Let us suppose that a receiver Re utilizes a sealed black box executable software $Al(\mathbf{r}, k)$ on a watermarked medium $\mathbf{r}$. The key k has been implemented by the watermarker inside Al and it is not an input to Al as $\mathbf{r}$ is. Figure 1 synthesizes the scenario in case Re, after having possibly downloaded both $\mathbf{r}$ and the executable software detector $Al(\mathbf{r}, k)$ into his DHN (Digital Home Network), operates at his DHN. Figure 2 synthesizes the same scenario but utilizes a remote site, where $Al(\mathbf{r}, k)$ is, of a wired network which offers the service. Analogously, in Figure 3 the service is offered by a node of a mobile ad hoc network.

We assume the untrustworthy scenario where Re becomes the attacker. Al outputs a binary decision answer a, on every input $\mathbf{r}$, by following a binary Hypothesis Testing decision procedure that utilizes a detection formula whose computational properties (as linearity, complexity, etc.) are overlooked here.

We distinguish the following detection channels in the previous figures. The channel between Re and Al, where $\mathbf{r}$ is sent as input to $Al(\mathbf{r}, k)$ and then

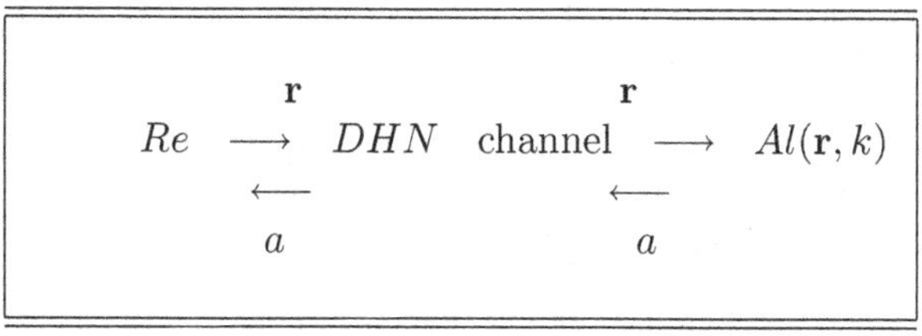

Fig. 1. $\mathbf{r}$ and $Al(\mathbf{r}, k)$ are at the DHN; $\mathbf{r}$ is the generic, either unmodified or modified, input to $Al(\mathbf{r}, k)$ through the DHN channel from Re to $Al(\mathbf{r}, k)$. The decision answer a by $Al(\mathbf{r}, k)$ on $\mathbf{r}$ is returned to Re through the DHN channel from $Al(\mathbf{r}, k)$ to Re.

$$Re \xrightarrow{\textbf{r}} wired\ \ network\ \ channel \xrightarrow{\textbf{r}} Al(\mathbf{r}, k)$$
$$\xleftarrow{} \qquad\qquad\qquad \xleftarrow{}$$
$$a \qquad\qquad\qquad\qquad\qquad a$$

Fig. 2. Executable software $Al(\mathbf{r}, k)$ is at a site of a wired network (for instance at the remote server of the creator of that software). $Al(\mathbf{r}, k)$ sends, through a wired network channel, its decision response on $\mathbf{r}$ as a binary output whose generic element is a, once $\mathbf{r}$ has been given as input to $Al(\mathbf{r}, k)$.

$$\odot \qquad\qquad\qquad \odot$$
$$\odot Re \xrightarrow{\textbf{r}} \odot wireless\ \ network\ \ channel \odot \xrightarrow{\textbf{r}} \odot Al(\mathbf{r}, k)$$
$$\xleftarrow{} \qquad\qquad\qquad \xleftarrow{}$$
$$a \qquad\qquad\qquad\qquad\qquad a$$

Fig. 3. Software $Al(\mathbf{r}, k)$ is at a node of a mobile network and sends its decision response a on the either unmodified or modified input $\mathbf{r}$ through nodes of a wireless ad hoc network

$a = Al(\mathbf{r}, k)$ is sent to Re. Such a channel is in the DHN of Re in Figure 1, in a wired network in Figure 2 and in a wireless ad hoc network in Figure 3. We term Q such a channel. We suppose that Q is noiseless. Let Q_n, with n having a finite range, $n = 1, ..., N$, $N \geq 2$, denote Q at its nth usage. Since Q is a noiseless channel, any transmitted decision answer $a = Al(\mathbf{r}, k)$, with a either 1 or 0 at each Q_n, is received without error. An information rate is achievable for Q. Re uses Al as an oracle. The information about the watermark leaks from the received response at usage n flowing through a $Q_{o,n}$ from Al to Re. An information rate is also achievable for covert channel $Q_o = \{Q_{o,n}\}$. We term *oracle channel* the channel Q_o in Q where the information exploited by Re leaks through.

Typical properties of an *oracle channel* are expressed in the following items i)-vi) which are correspondent to the items for classical covert channels we have pointed out in the Introduction.

i) There is no malicious sender. Re is the unique attacker. Sender Al does not collaborate, under a predetermined agreement, with Re to set up and maintain Q_o. Al simply helps Re as long as it outputs answers on inputs sent by Re.

ii) Q_o is not foreseen by the watermarking scheme designer.

iii) Q_o violates the Q security.
iv) Q_o is difficult to detect.
v) Short answers characterize channel Q_o.
vi) Secret information is leaked rather than sent/received.

Clearly, oracle channels differ from classical covert channels.

4   Counteracting Oracle Channels

In order to counteract oracle attacks, the authors of [20,21] propose:

1. A decision interval, i.e. two thresholds thr and Thr, with $thr < Thr$. Any detection value below thr denotes that the watermark misses. Any detection value above Thr denotes that the proper watermark is present. Within the interval $[thr, Thr]$, values become 0 or 1 randomly, based on the pdf of a squared *sine* function.
2. Non-linear ingredients in the detection formula.
   Such a line is also in [30,31] and, more effectively, in [32] where a fractal decision boundary (as for instance the Peano curve) has been exploited.

We propose that in order to counteract Re in getting secret information, the scheme designer can modify algorithm Al so as Al gets a memory as a storing location for hashed versions of its inputs. Specifically, as an alternative to suitable communication protocols, that necessarily involve protected connections for the interactive behavior of the involved parties, the scheme designer can counteract a possible unknown channel Q_o of a known channel Q by acting on Q *via* a modification of algorithm $Al(\mathbf{r}, k)$.

Here we formulate three methods to modify $Al(\mathbf{r}, k)$ into algorithm $Al_i(\mathbf{r}, k)$, $i = 1, 2, 3$, having a hash table μ_i as its own memory. Thus channels Q, Q_o become channels Q_i, $Q_{i,o}$, respectively.

Let us premise the hash table definition that shall be utilized in Section 5.

4.1   Hash Tables for Values of Stable Hash Functions

Hash functions have been used for data indexing and for detecting data manipulation. In order to guarantee that it is difficult to find $\mathbf{y} \neq \mathbf{x}$ such that $h(\mathbf{y}) = h(\mathbf{x})$, a traditional hash function $h(.)$ is not *stable* in the sense that even if $\mathbf{y}$ is obtained from $\mathbf{x}$ by a small change, $h(\mathbf{y})$ is very different from $h(\mathbf{x})$. Known cryptographic hash functions are not *stable*. Nowadays, it is widely recognized that digital media most often require soft hashing in the sense that a hash function is *stable* in a neighbor of its input (e.g. the *perceptual hash functions* as reviewed in [33]).

As *stable hash functions* we take the *similarity preserving hash functions* in [34]. Choosing a random vector $\mathbf{ran}$ from the $L_{u,v}$-dimensional Gaussian distribution, where $L_{u,v}$ is the common length of vectors $\mathbf{u}$ and $\mathbf{v}$, a hash function $h_{\mathbf{ran}}(\mathbf{u})$ is defined as follows:

$$h_{\mathbf{ran}}(\mathbf{u}) = \begin{cases} 1 \text{ if } \mathbf{ran} \cdot \mathbf{u} \geq 0 \\ 0 \text{ if } \mathbf{ran} \cdot \mathbf{u} < 0 \end{cases}$$

where the product between **ran** and **u** is the scalar product. For a family of *similarity preserving hash functions* the probability that $h_{\mathbf{ran}}(\mathbf{u}) = h_{\mathbf{ran}}(\mathbf{v})$ is as follows:

$$P(h_{\mathbf{ran}}(\mathbf{u}) = h_{\mathbf{ran}}(\mathbf{v})) = |1 - \frac{\theta(\mathbf{u}, \mathbf{v})}{\pi}| \tag{1}$$

where $\theta(\mathbf{u}, \mathbf{v})$ is the angle between **u** and **v** computed by $\theta(\cdot, \cdot)$ that takes values in $[0, \pi]$. The similarity function $sim(\mathbf{u}, \mathbf{v}) = |1 - \frac{\theta(\mathbf{u},\mathbf{v})}{\pi}|$ maps pairs of vectors **u**, **v** to a real number in the interval $[0, 1]$. The extreme values 0 and 1 are obtained as follows:

$$sim(\mathbf{u}, \mathbf{v}) = |1 - \frac{\theta(\mathbf{u}, \mathbf{v})}{\pi}| = \begin{cases} 1 \text{ if } \mathbf{u} \text{ and } \mathbf{v} \text{ are identical} \\ 0 \text{ if } \mathbf{u} \text{ and } \mathbf{v} \text{ have opposite directions} \end{cases} \tag{2}$$

Since the output of each $h_{\mathbf{ran}}(.)$ is one bit, by concatenating the output of t such hash functions, the following hash functions composed of t bits

$$\begin{cases} h(\mathbf{u}) = h_{\mathbf{ran}_1}(\mathbf{u}) \ldots h_{\mathbf{ran}_t}(\mathbf{u}) \\ h(\mathbf{v}) = h_{\mathbf{ran}_1}(\mathbf{v}) \ldots h_{\mathbf{ran}_t}(\mathbf{v}) \end{cases}$$

are obtained. Similarity of such binary strings can be measured by the *Extended Hamming Distance*, d_{EHD}, as for instance in [35] with a threshold δ. The error probability $P_e(h(\mathbf{u}) = h(\mathbf{v}) \mid \mathbf{u} \neq \mathbf{v})$ is negligible as soon as it is below a predetermined threshold in $[0, 1]$.

A *hash table* can be used to store the results of a similarity preserving hash function $h(.)$. Hash tables [36] are used to efficiently perform search, insertion and removal of values by means of an *access function* H, that is a specific hash function for hash table lookup which associates each elements of a set with a position (the *hash address*) of the table, say in $1, \ldots, M$. Often such an access function H is the composition of two functions: the first function associates a binary string to an integer; the second associates an integer to one position of the table, i.e. to an integer in $1, \ldots, M$. An efficient handling of collisions is fundamental for hash tables. Figure 4 shows a typical hash table, where each

1	$h(\mathbf{x})$
2	$h(\mathbf{y})$
3	0
4	$h(\mathbf{u})$
	⋮
10	$h(\mathbf{z})$
11	0
	⋮
M	0

Fig. 4. Typical hash table with addresses from 1 to M

location is either empty, and then contains the null element 0, or contains a hash value obtained by $h(.)$.

5   The Methods

To formulate the methods we propose, we write $h(\mathbf{r}) \in \mu_i$ to express that some $h(\mathbf{u})$ is within μ_i such that $d_{EHD}(h(\mathbf{r}), h(\mathbf{u})) < \delta$, i.e. $h(\mathbf{r})$ approximately matches with $h(\mathbf{u})$.

For vector $\mathbf{r}$ as input, first of all each $Al_i(\mathbf{r}, k)$ has to verify whether there exists some hashed vector $h(\mathbf{u})$ within μ_i which approximately matches with $h(\mathbf{r})$, being $\mathbf{u}$ a previous input to Al_i. Then Al_i continues to work accordingly.

Having memory μ_i a finite dimension, every Al_i deletes a stored $h(\mathbf{r})$ from its full hash table following a suitable strategy. Let Δ_i represent the average time interval during which $h(\mathbf{r})$ remains in memory μ_i. Δ_i depends on the (secret) dimension of μ_i. Resizing the hash table can be exploited to cope with such a removal problem.

5.1   Method 1

By Method 1 algorithm Al is modified into algorithm Al_1.

Algorithm Al_1 increases randomness in the sense that Al_1 returns also random bits $\underline{a}$, with $\underline{a} \in \{\underline{1}, \underline{0}\}$ as its decision responses. We denote by $\underline{1}$, $\underline{0}$ randomly generated numbers 1, 0, respectively. Specifically, Al_1 randomizes its decision responses on suitable inputs only. To this aim $Al_1(\mathbf{r}, k) \in \{a, \underline{a}\}$, works as follows:

i) if $h(\mathbf{r}) \notin \mu_1$, then $Al_1(\mathbf{r}, k)$ works as $Al(\mathbf{r}, k)$ and then stores $h(\mathbf{r})$ in μ_1;
ii) if $h(\mathbf{r}) \in \mu_1$, then $Al_1(\mathbf{r}, k)$ stores $h(\mathbf{r})$ in μ_1 and returns 0 or 1 randomly.

We do not address here random/pseudo-random bit generation. We allow different techniques to be possibly used in Al_1 and allow to follow a secret distribution chosen by the designer. We suppose that Al_1 does not take into account time duration.

5.2   Method 2

By Method 2 algorithm Al is modified into algorithm Al_2.

Method 2 takes into account the time durations of decision answers. We suppose that decision answers by Al_2 take a time duration that can be different even for the same answer on the same input, in case it is repeated. Algorithm Al_2 is designed to honor the following temporal constraint.

The Temporal Constraint - Let $|Al_2(\mathbf{r}, k)|_{Q_{2,n}}$ stand for the time duration of the response given by Al_2 at the channel usage $Q_{2,n}$ and $n = 1, ..., N$.

The desired temporal constraint can be expressed, for signals $\mathbf{r}$, $\mathbf{r}'$, as

$$|Al_2(\mathbf{r}', k)|_{Q_{2,m+j}} > |Al_2(\mathbf{r}, k)|_{Q_{2,m}} \quad if \quad d_{EHD}(h(\mathbf{r}), h(\mathbf{r}')) \leq \delta \qquad (3)$$

for $j \geq 1$, $m = 1, ..., N$ and $Q_{2,m}, Q_{2,m+j} \in \{Q_{2,n}\}$.

Thus $\mathbf{r}'$ is an input to Al_2 within the average time interval Δ_2 during which $h(\mathbf{r})$ remains in memory μ_2.

To take time duration into account, we write $*a$ to mean that a is delayed. The delay duration is here denoted as $|*| = c$. $Al_2(\mathbf{r}, k) \in \{a, *a\}$ works as follows:

i) if $h(\mathbf{r}) \notin \mu_2$, then $Al_2(\mathbf{r}, k)$ works as $Al(\mathbf{r}, k)$ and then stores $h(\mathbf{r})$ in μ_2;
ii) if $h(\mathbf{r}) \in \mu_2$, then $Al_2(\mathbf{r}, k)$ stores $h(\mathbf{r})$ in μ_2 and returns $*a$. This means that Al_2 delays its response a on $\mathbf{r}$, specifically that Al_2 answers after c time units. The c's values can be tuned to obtain the desired time delay.

5.3   Method 3

By Method 3 algorithm Al is modified into algorithm Al_3.

Method 3 increases randomness as well as delays its decision responses. $Al_3(\mathbf{r}, k) \in \{a, *\underline{a}\}$, works as follows:

i) if $h(\mathbf{r}) \notin \mu_3$, then $Al_3(\mathbf{r}, k)$ works as $Al(\mathbf{r}, k)$ and then stores $h(\mathbf{r})$ in μ_3;
ii) if $h(\mathbf{r}) \in \mu_3$, then $Al_3(\mathbf{r}, k)$, stores $h(\mathbf{r})$ in μ_3 and returns $*\underline{a}$, i.e. $Al_3(\mathbf{r}, k)$ answers 0 or 1 randomly after c time units.

Therefore decision answers by Al_3 take a different time duration as long as Al_3 behaves as Al_2.

5.4   Computational Overhead

The computational overhead each Al_i suffers with respect to Al consists of the creation and management of hash table memory μ_i. We can state that nonetheless the *network cost* does not significantly increase because:

- for what concerns storage, although it is not a major cost for a network, the increase is not significant since the dimension of hash tables has not to be large in order to be practical;
- for what concerns management, the used hash functions should map most of the signals onto unique integers, i.e. the number of collisions should be sufficiently small, and thus $O(1)$ search time is realistic for elements stored in the hash table. Otherwise, collisions are handled in an efficient manner [36]. We do not detail here on this subject matter. Also possible hash table resizing can be performed in an efficient manner.

6   Trade-Off between Counteracting and Detection Reliability

Here we analyze the trade-off between the success of each algorithm Al_i to counteract information leakage and the Al_i detection reliability as defined in the Hypothesis Testing setting.

Let us suppose that the attacker uses an Al_i, $i = 1, 2, 3$, as a sealed black box, instead of Al, to perform an oracle attack. Let α_i be the obtained sequence of responses instead of sequence α obtained under Al. We suppose that each request by the attacker occurs within the time interval Δ_i related to the hash table μ_i, and therefore α_i is obtained from media whose hashed versions are in the memory of Al_i.

Point i) of Propositions 1, 2 and 3 show that the proposed countermeasures are adequate. However, the following *caveat* arises:

Caveat: Al_i, $i = 1, 2, 3$, *might be less reliable than Al when no oracle attack is being performed.*

In fact, there may be a hashed value in memory μ_i of Al_i, $i = 1, 2, 3$, such that an approximate match is found in the hash table for some $\mathbf{r}$.

Point ii) of Propositions 1, 2 and 3 show that each Al_i has practically the same reliability Al has when no oracle attack is performed.

An information-theoretic perspective has been widely followed in steganography and watermarking, as e.g. in [37] among others. To make this paper self-contained, we adapt to our context the basic information-theoretic notions [38,39] we utilize. Let $\mathbf{X}$, $\mathbf{W}$, $\mathbf{Y}$ and $\mathbf{R}$ be discrete vector-valued random variables for the original host signal, the watermark, the watermarked signal and the signal which is input to the detector, respectively. Let medium $\mathbf{r}$, the watermarked $\mathbf{y} = \mathbf{x}[\mathbf{w}]$, watermark $\mathbf{w}$ and medium $\mathbf{x}$ be a generic realization of $\mathbf{R}$, $\mathbf{Y}$, $\mathbf{W}$ and $\mathbf{X}$, respectively. We suppose that $\mathbf{w}$ is not a deterministic function of $\mathbf{x}$ or $\mathbf{y}$ or $\mathbf{r}$. The independence between $\mathbf{W}$ and $\mathbf{R}$ is globally stated about their probability distributions as $p_{\mathbf{WR}} = p_{\mathbf{W}}.p_{\mathbf{R}}$, where $p_{\mathbf{WR}}$ is the joint probability distribution (i.e. $p_{\mathbf{WR}} = P(\mathbf{W} = \mathbf{w}, \mathbf{R} = \mathbf{r})$) and $p_{\mathbf{W}}.p_{\mathbf{R}}$ the product of the two marginal distributions $p_{\mathbf{W}}$, $p_{\mathbf{R}}$. The distance from the independence condition between $\mathbf{W}$ and $\mathbf{R}$ can be measured by the *Kullback-Leibler distance* (or *relative entropy* or *information discrimination*) that defines the *mutual information* $I(\mathbf{W}; \mathbf{R})$ between $\mathbf{W}$ and $\mathbf{R}$ as

$$D(p_{\mathbf{WR}}//p_{\mathbf{W}}.p_{\mathbf{R}}) = \sum_{\mathbf{w},\mathbf{r}} p(\mathbf{w}, \mathbf{r}) log \frac{p(\mathbf{w}, \mathbf{r})}{p(\mathbf{w}).p(\mathbf{r})} =_{def} I(\mathbf{W}; \mathbf{R}) \qquad (4)$$

with $p(\mathbf{w}, \mathbf{r}) > 0$ and $p(\mathbf{w}).p(\mathbf{r}) \geq 0$. The information-discrimination is a pseudo-distance. In general it has no upper bound and it is asymmetric. $I(\mathbf{W}; \mathbf{R}) \geq 0$ and is symmetric. If $\mathbf{W}$ is a deterministic function of $\mathbf{R}$, or $\mathbf{R}$ is of $\mathbf{W}$, then $I(\mathbf{W}; \mathbf{R}) = 0$.

A communication channel is characterized by a probability transition matrix that determines, given the input, the conditional distribution of the output. Capacity is one of its basic properties. As pointed out already in [3], having capacity an asymptotic character, it is fine for very long files or documents sent over a long period of time. It has been shown that existing watermarking systems operate far below capacity. We will not address capacity anymore in the sequel.

The mutual information between $\mathbf{W}$ and itself, $I(\mathbf{W}; \mathbf{W})$, that expectably is the maximum value of dependence, is obtained from (4) as [38]

$$I(\mathbf{W}; \mathbf{W}) =_{def} H(\mathbf{W}). \qquad (5)$$

The *conditional entropy* $H(\mathbf{W}|\mathbf{R})$ is the uncertainty associated with $\mathbf{W}$ given $\mathbf{R}$. Since

$$H(\mathbf{W}) \geq H(\mathbf{W}|\mathbf{R}) \tag{6}$$

adding condition variables possibly leads to decrease entropy on the average. Equality holds if variables are stochastically independent of one another. From

$$I(\mathbf{W};\mathbf{R}) = H(\mathbf{W}) + H(\mathbf{R}) - H(\mathbf{W},\mathbf{R}) = H(\mathbf{W}) - H(\mathbf{W}|\mathbf{R})$$

since $H(\mathbf{W},\mathbf{R}) = H(\mathbf{W}|\mathbf{R}) + H(\mathbf{R})$, $I(\mathbf{W};\mathbf{R})$ is the reduction in uncertainty concerning $\mathbf{W}$ due to $\mathbf{R}$, i.e. the reduction in entropy that $\mathbf{R}$ provides about $\mathbf{W}$.

Let $\mathcal{A} = \mathcal{A}_N = (A_1,\ldots,A_N)$ be a decision response finite sequence of binary random variables whose generic element is simply denoted as A. Let $\alpha = \alpha_N = (a_1,\ldots,a_N)$ be a sequence of generic realizations of the random variables in $\mathcal{A}$ such that $a_1 = Al(\mathbf{r}_1,k)$, $a_2 = Al(\mathbf{r}_2,k)$, $\ldots$, $a_N = Al(\mathbf{r}_N,k)$. Decision responses are obtained by statistical binary Hypothesis Testing (that is a steganalysis procedure [40,41,42]). Therefore α may contain some wrong answers, under a suitable decision threshold.

Let $\mathcal{R} = \mathcal{R}_N = (\mathbf{R}_1,\ldots,\mathbf{R}_N)$ be a finite sequence of discrete vector-valued random variables whose generic element is simply denoted as R. Let $\rho = \rho_N = (\mathbf{r}_1,\ldots,\mathbf{r}_N)$ be a finite media sequence of generic realizations of the random variables in $\mathcal{R}$, i.e. $\mathbf{r}$ is the generic realization of $\mathbf{R}$ such that $\mathbf{r}_{N+1}$ is obtained by the attacker performing modifications on $\mathbf{r}_N$, after having observed both $\mathbf{r}_N$ and a_N. Then we consider $H(\mathbf{W}|\mathbf{R},A)$ with

$$H(\mathbf{W}|\mathbf{R},A) = H(\mathbf{W}|\mathbf{R}) - H(A|\mathbf{R}). \tag{7}$$

$I(\mathbf{W};\mathbf{R},A) > 0$, with

$$I(\mathbf{W};\mathbf{R},A) = H(\mathbf{W}) - H(\mathbf{W}|\mathbf{R},A) \tag{8}$$

has to be minimized for the secrecy issue, provided that the watermark is not a deterministic function of the host content.

The Shannon's perfect secrecy for $\mathbf{W}$ on $I(\mathbf{W};\mathbf{R},A)$ requires $I(\mathbf{W};\mathbf{R},A) = 0$, that can be approximated if $\mathbf{W}$ and pair $(\mathbf{R},A)$ can be considered as stochastically independent of one another. However, this is not realistic outside degenerate cases and therefore the hopefully minimized $I(\mathbf{W};\mathbf{R},A)$ is positive such that it cannot be approximated to zero.

6.1   Performance of Method 1

For what concerns Method 1, Proposition 1 holds.

Proposition 1. *Under algorithm Al_1 used as a sealed black box,*

i) *during an oracle attack, the mutual information $I(\mathbf{W};\mathbf{R},A)$ under Al_1 at step $N \geq 2$ is less than the one under Al;*

ii) *Al_1 is less reliable than Al during an oracle attack;*

iii) *without performing an oracle attack, detection reliability under Al_1 and that under Al are practically the same.*

<u>Proof</u> - **i)** The finite sequence of the generic decision answers by Al_1 until the current step $N \geq 2$ can be written as follows:

$$\alpha_1 = \alpha_{1,N} = (a_{1,1}, a_{1,2}, \ldots, a_{1,N}) = (a, \underline{a}, \ldots, \underline{a})$$

where the first element $a = Al_1(\mathbf{r}_1, k) = Al(\mathbf{r}_1, k)$ is the generic answer on the original $\mathbf{r}_1$; the second element is the random answer on the modified $\mathbf{r}_1$; and so on.

Let $A_{1,N}$ be the random variable whose generic realization is $a_{1,N}$. We have to show that, at step $N \geq 2$, $I(\mathbf{W}; \mathbf{R}_{1,N}, A_{1,N}) < I(\mathbf{W}; \mathbf{R}_N, A_N)$, where $\mathbf{R}_{1,N}$ is $\mathbf{R}_N$ relative to Al_1.

Since, for $N \geq 2$, $A_{1,N}$ is 'more random' than A_N because the probability to be random for $a_{1,N}$ is greater than zero while the probability to be random for a_N is zero,

$$H(\mathbf{W}|\mathbf{R}_{1,N}, A_{1,N}) \geq H(\mathbf{W}|\mathbf{R}_N, A_N)$$

From (8),

$$I(\mathbf{W}; \mathbf{R}_{1,N}, A_{1,N}) = H(\mathbf{W}) - H(\mathbf{W}|\mathbf{R}_{1,N}, A_{1,N})$$

and

$$I(\mathbf{W}; \mathbf{R}_N, A_N) = H(\mathbf{W}) - H(\mathbf{W}|\mathbf{R}_N, A_N)$$

hold and therefore

$$I(\mathbf{W}; \mathbf{R}_{1,N}, A_{1,N}) \leq I(\mathbf{W}; \mathbf{R}_N, A_N)$$

with

$$I(\mathbf{W}; \mathbf{R}_{1,N}, A_{1,N}) < I(\mathbf{W}; \mathbf{R}_N, A_N)$$

in non-degenerated scenarios.   ◇

ii) During an oracle attack, Al_1 is obviously less reliable than Al because of its greater randomness that increases the error probability of its decision responses.   ◇

iii) Under the assumption that the error probability of hash functions is negligible, α_1 is a sequence obtained on signals in ρ_1 very few of which have their hash version that match with elements in μ_1. This entails that Al_1 has practically the same detection reliability Al has when no attack occurs since it gives the same answers on the same inputs. Thus for A_N, $A_{1,N}$ with probability distributions $p_{A_N}, p_{A_{1,N}}$; $\mathbf{R}_N$, $\mathbf{R}_{1,N}$ with probability distributions $p_{\mathbf{R}_N}$, $p_{\mathbf{R}_{1,N}}$

$$D(p_{A_{1,N}}//p_{A_N}) \sim 0 \text{ and } D(p_{\mathbf{R}_{1,N}}//p_{\mathbf{R}_N}) \sim 0$$

and

$$I(\mathbf{W}; \mathbf{R}_{1,N}, A_{1,N}) \sim I(\mathbf{W}; \mathbf{R}_N, A_N) \text{ ◇}$$

6.2   Performance of Method 2

Time duration of the decision responses is basic for Method 2. Let $|a| = t > 0$ denote the time duration, measured by the assumed time unit, to obtain decision response a by Al. Let $E\{t\}$ be the expected value of t. For channels that work interactively and are effective if the time duration of responses is reasonable, as oracle channels do, time duration of the decision response is a relevant notion to be taken into account also at the information-theoretic setting.

The Temporal Mutual Information - The *temporal mutual information*, $I_t(\mathbf{W}; \mathbf{R}, A)$, relates information leakage with the time duration of the decision response. In [3] the temporal capacity is defined. Here we define the *temporal mutual information* $I_t(\mathbf{W}; \mathbf{R}, A)$ as follows

$$I_t(\mathbf{W}; \mathbf{R}, A) = \frac{I(\mathbf{W}; \mathbf{R}, A)}{E\{t\}}. \tag{9}$$

The time response of Al at the denominator of (9) makes $I_t(\mathbf{W}; \mathbf{R}, A)$ to decrease as $E\{t\}$ increases. If the temporal mutual information decreases then the information rate also decreases.

For what concerns Method 2, Proposition 2 holds.

Proposition 2. *Under algorithm Al_2 used as a sealed black box,*

i) *the temporal mutual information under Al_2 at step $N \geq 2$ is less than the one under Al during an oracle attack;*

ii) *Al_2 is reliable as Al is during an oracle attack;*

iii) *without performing an oracle attack, detection reliability under Al_2 and that under Al are practically the same.*

Proof - i) The finite sequence of the generic decision answers by Al_2 until step N can be written as follows:

$$\alpha_2 = \alpha_{2,N} = (a_{2,1}, a_{2,2}, \ldots, a_{2,N}) = (a, *a, \ldots, *a)$$

where the first element $a = Al_2(\mathbf{r}_1, k) = Al(\mathbf{r}_1, k)$ is the generic answer on the original $\mathbf{r} = \mathbf{r}_1$; the second element is the answer on $\mathbf{r}_2$ that is the modified $\mathbf{r}_1$, and so on.

Let $A_{2,N}$ be the random variable whose generic realization is $a_{2,N}$. We have to show that, at step $N \geq 2$, $I_t(\mathbf{W}; \mathbf{R}_{2,N}, A_{2,N}) < I_t(\mathbf{W}; \mathbf{R}_N, A_N)$, where $\mathbf{R}_{2,N}$ and $\mathbf{R}_N$ are practically the same.

Since $t_{2,N} = |a_{2,N}| > |a_N|$, because $a_{2,N}$ differs from a_N only because of $*$ whose meaning is delay, the expected value $E\{t_{2,N}\}$ is such that

$$E\{t_{2,N}\} > E\{t_N\}$$

while

$$I(\mathbf{W}; \mathbf{R}_{2,N}, A_{2,N}) = I(\mathbf{W}; \mathbf{R}_N, A_N).$$

Then

$$I_t(\mathbf{W}; \mathbf{R}_N, A_N) = \frac{I(\mathbf{W}; \mathbf{R}_N, A_N)}{E\{t_N\}} > \frac{I(\mathbf{W}; \mathbf{R}_{2,N}, A_{2,N})}{E\{t_{2,N}\}} = I_t(\mathbf{W}; \mathbf{R}_{2,N}, A_{2,N}) \diamond$$

ii) Under the assumption that the error probability of the used hash functions are negligible, every α_2 is a sequence obtained on signals in ρ_2 very few of which have their hash versions that match with elements in μ_2. This entails that Al_2 has obviously the same detection reliability Al has also during an oracle attack as an immediate consequence of the fact that Al_2 returns exactly the same decision responses of Al on the same inputs, possibly at a delayed time instant. $\diamond$
iii) Under the assumption that the error probability of hash functions is negligible, Al_2 has practically the same detection reliability Al has when no attack occurs since it gives the same answers on the same inputs. Thus for A_N, $A_{2,N}$ with probability distributions p_{A_N}, $p_{A_{2,N}}$; $\mathbf{R}_N$, $\mathbf{R}_{2,N}$ with probability distributions $p_{\mathbf{R}_N}$, $p_{\mathbf{R}_{2,N}}$, as in point iii) of Proposition 1, at a greater extent

$$D(p_{A_{2,N}} // p_{A_N}) \sim 0 \text{ and } D(p_{\mathbf{R}_{2,N}} // p_{\mathbf{R}_N}) \sim 0$$

and

$$I(\mathbf{W}; \mathbf{R}_{2,N}, A_{2,N}) \sim I(\mathbf{W}; \mathbf{R}_N, A_N) \diamond$$

6.3 Performance of Method 3

For what concerns Method 3, Proposition 3 holds as a Corollary of Proposition 1 and Proposition 2.

Proposition 3. *Under algorithm Al_3 used as a sealed black box,*

i) *during an oracle attack, the temporal mutual information at step $N \geq 2$ is less than the one under Al;*
ii) *Al_3 is less reliable than Al during an oracle attack;*
iii) *without performing an oracle attack, detection reliability under Al_3 and that under Al are practically the same.*

<u>Proof</u> - **i)** We have to show that $I_t(\mathbf{W}; \mathbf{R}_{3,N}, A_{3,N}) < I_t(\mathbf{W}; \mathbf{R}_N, A_N)$, where $\mathbf{R}_{3,N}$ is modified by Al_3. In the following sequence

$$\alpha_3 = \alpha_{3,N} = (a_{3,1}, a_{3,2}, \dots, a_{3,N}) = (a, *\underline{a}, \dots, *\underline{a})$$

the first element $a = Al_3(\mathbf{r}_1, k) = Al(\mathbf{r}_1, k)$ is the answer on the original $\mathbf{r} = \mathbf{r}_1$, the second element is the answer on the modified $\mathbf{r}_1$, and so on.

Let $A_{3,N}$ be the random variable whose generic realization is $a_{3,N}$. Now under Al_3 the temporal mutual information decreases, at step $N \geq 2$, because in

$$I_t(\mathbf{W}; \mathbf{R}_N, A_N) = \frac{I(\mathbf{W}; \mathbf{R}_N, A_N)}{E\{t_N\}} > \frac{I(\mathbf{W}; \mathbf{R}_{3,N}, A_{3,N})}{E\{t_{3,N}\}} = I_t(\mathbf{W}; \mathbf{R}_{3,N}, A_{3,N})$$

the numerator decreases under Al_3 as under Al_1 and the denominator increases under Al_3 as under Al_2. $\diamond$

ii) During an oracle attack, Al_3 is obviously less reliable than Al at the same extent Al_1 is.   ⋄

iii) Al_3 has practically the same reliability Al has when no attack occurs as a consequence of item iii) of Proposition 1 and of Proposition 2.   ⋄

7   Conclusions and Further Work

Oracle attacks have been shown in this paper to be new covert channels, we term oracle channels. This helped us to propose modification methods for watermarking detection algorithms so as to face how to contrast possible oracle channels at the very formulation phase of watermarking schemes. An important aspect of our proposals is that they aim reducing information leakage at a low *network cost*. Information-theoretic notions allow us to prove that the modified algorithms that can be obtained by the proposed methods do enhance security with respect to oracle attacks and moreover their detection reliability is practically the same in case no oracle attack is performed. However, for what concerns Method 1 and Method 3, a good reliability does not allow increasing randomness to a degree such that the mutual information becomes negligible.

As a consequence of Propositions 1, 2 and 3, during an oracle attack, the diminution of the information leakage for channel Q_i, $i = 1, 2, 3$, with respect to that of Q, entails an information rate decrease of oracle channel $Q_{i,o}$ with respect to that of oracle channel Q_o.

The proposed methods are designed to work under the usual assumption of one attacker who disposes of one detector with one chosen medium as input. If this is not the case, different actual scenarios are in order. Let us consider the following two strategies (suggested to us by a Referee) an attacker could follow to nullify the countermeasures here proposed.

Case 1. Oracle attack using different detectors
    To cope with such a case, some technique of collaborating algorithms on the same data structure should be exploited. For instance, different detector copies made by one attacker, could be forced, at the implementation level, to share the same hash memory if they are copies that are stored in a peer-to-peer network or in the same network device. Otherwise, different detectors with different hash memories should be stored in different subnetworks and should require different attackers who communicate and collaborate each other. Such a scenario should require a relevant computation or communication overhead.

Case 2. Oracle attack with several contents, feeding them to the detector in such a way that when the attacked version of a content is input again to the detector, its hash was already removed from the memory.
    To cope with such a case, a new larger table is built up [36], whenever, at the implementation setting, the previously designed table turns out to be soon dramatically inadequate. The total cost is $O(M)$ because all the contents of the original table, whose size is M, are added to the new table. If enlarging

the hash table all at once may interrupt time-critical operations, resizing has to be gradual. (For instance, a new hash table can be allocated without deallocation of the old one, and both tables are checked during lookups, for a while. Each new insertion is performed into the new table together with also the insertion of some element of the old table. Finally the old table is deallocated when all elements are removed from it.)

Linear hashing permits incremental hash table expansion. *Consistent hashing* decreases the resizing cost by using access hash functions such that the addresses of most values do not change when the table is resized.

References

1. Simmons, G.J.: Subliminal Channels: Past and Present. European Trans. on Telecommunications 5(4), 459–473 (1994)
2. Millen, J.: 20 years of covert channel modeling and analysis. In: Proceedings of Symposium on Security and Privacy, pp. 113–114. IEEE Computer Society Press, Los Alamitos (1999)
3. Moskowitz, I., Kang, M.: Covert channels - here to stay. In: Proceedings of COMPASS 1994, pp. 235–243. IEEE, Los Alamitos (1994)
4. Lampson, B.W.: A Note on the Confinement Problem. Comm. ACM 16, 613–615 (1973)
5. Provos, N., Honeyman, P.: Detecting Steganographic Content on the Internet. IEEE Trans. on Information Theory 49(3), 563–593 (2003)
6. Tumoian, E., Anikeev, M.: Network Based Detection of Passive Covert Channels in TCP/IP. In: Proceedings of the IEEE Conference on Local Computer Networks 30th Anniversary, pp. 802–809. IEEE, Los Alamitos (2005)
7. Ahsan, K., Kundur, D.: Practical Data hiding in TCP/IP. In: Proceedings of Workshop on multimedia Security at ACM Multimedia 2002, ACM Press, New York (2002)
8. Servetto, S.D., Vetterli, M.: Communication Using Phantoms: Covert Channels in the Internet. In: Proceedings IEEE International Symposium on Information Theory (ISIT), USA (2001)
9. Li, S., Ephremides, A.: A Network Layer Covert Channel in Ad-hoc Wireless Networks. In: Proceedings of Int. Conf. on Image Processing 1998 (ICIP 1998), vol. 1, pp. 88–96. IEEE, Los Alamitos (2004)
10. Shnayder, V.: Opportunities for Language Based Information Flow Security in Sensor Networks (2004)
11. Kocher, P.C.: Timing attacks on implementations of Diffie-Hellman, RSA, DSS, and other systems. In: Koblitz, N. (ed.) CRYPTO 1996. LNCS, vol. 1109, pp. 104–113. Springer, Heidelberg (1996)
12. Jajodia, S., Meadows, C.: Inference Problems in Multilevel Secure Database Management Systems. Information Security 570–585 (1991)
13. Zeng, W., Lan, J., Zhuang, X.: Network friendly media security: rationales, solutions and open issues. In: Proceedings IEEE Int. Conf. on Image Processing (ICIP 2004), IEEE, Singapore (2004)
14. Barni, M., Bartolini, F., Furon, T.: A general framework for robust watermarking security. Signal Processing, Elsevier, special issue on Security of Data Hiding Technologies, vol. 83, pp. 2069–2084 (invited paper) (2003)

15. Barni, M., Bartolini, F.: Watermarking Systems Engineering: Enabling Digital Assets Security and other Applications. Dekker Inc (2004)

16. Cayre, F., Fontaine, C., Furon, T.: Watermarking security part I: Theory. In: Delp, E.J., Wong, P.W. (eds.) Proc. SPIE-IS&T Electronic Imaging. SPIE, San Jose, CA, USA (2005)

17. Cayre, F., Fontaine, C., Furon, T.: Watermarking security part II: Practice. In: Delp, E.J., Wong, P.W. (eds.) Proc. SPIE-IST Electronic Imaging. SPIE, San Jose, CA, USA (2005)

18. Furon, T.: A survey of watermarking security. In: Barni, M., Cox, I., Kalker, T., Kim, H.J. (eds.) IWDW 2005. LNCS, vol. 3710, pp. 201–215. Springer, Heidelberg (2005)

19. Fridrich, J., Goljan, M.: Practical steganalysis of digital images: state of the art. In: Proceedings of SPIE Photonics West, vol. 4675, pp. 1–13 (2002)

20. Linnartz, J.-P., van Dijk, M.: Analysis of the sensitivity attack against electronic watermarks in images. In: Aucsmith, D. (ed.) IH 1998. LNCS, vol. 1525, pp. 258–272. Springer, Heidelberg (1998)

21. Kalker, T., Linnartz, J.-P., van Dijk, M.: Watermark estimation through detector analysis. In: Proc. of Int. Conf. on Image Processing 1998 (ICIP 1998), vol. 1, pp. 425–429. IEEE, Los Alamitos (1998)

22. Choubassi, M.E., Moulin, P.: New sensitivity analysis attack. In: Proceedings of International Symposium on Electronic Imaging, Security and Watermarking of Multimedia Contents VII. IS&T/SPIE, pp. 734–745 (2005)

23. Comesana, P., Perez-Freire, L., Perez-Gonzalez, F.: The Return of the Sensitivity Attack. In: Barni, M., Cox, I., Kalker, T., Kim, H.J. (eds.) IWDW 2005. LNCS, vol. 3710, pp. 260–274. Springer, Heidelberg (2005)

24. Perez-Freire, L., Comesana-Alfaro, P., Perez-Gonzales, F.: Detection in quantization-based watermarking: performance and security issues. In: Proceedings of International Symposium on Electronic Imaging, Security and Watermarking of Multimedia Contents VII. IS&T/SPIE, pp. 721–733 (2005)

25. Venturini, I.: Counteracting oracle attacks. In: Proc. of the Multimedia and Security Work. 2004 (MM and Sec 2004), pp. 187–192. ACM Press, Magdeburg, Germany (2004)

26. Venturini, I.: Oracle attacks and covert channels. In: Barni, M., Cox, I., Kalker, T., Kim, H.J. (eds.) IWDW 2005. LNCS, vol. 3710, pp. 171–185. Springer, Heidelberg (2005)

27. Cox, I., Miller, M., Bloom, J.: Digital Watermarking. Morgan Kaufmann Pub., Academic Press (2002)

28. Moulin, P., O'Sullivan, J.: Information-theoretic analysis of watermarking. In: Proc. of Int. Conf. on Acoustics, Speech and Signal Processing (ICASSP 2000), IEEE, Los Alamitos (2000)

29. Moulin, P., O'Sullivan, J.: Information-theoretic analysis of information hiding. IEEE Trans. on Information Theory 49(3), 563–593 (2003)

30. Furon, T., Venturini, I., Duhamel, P.: An unified approach of asymmetric watermarking schemes. In: Proceedings of International Symposium on Electronic Imaging, Security and Watermarking of Multimedia Contents III. IS&T/SPIE, pp. 269–279 (2001)

31. Furon, T., Macq, B., Hurley, B., Silvestre, G.: JANIS: Just Another N-order side-Informed watermarking Scheme. In: Proceedings of IEEE International Conf. on Image Processing, ICIP 2002, vol. 3, pp. 153–156. IEEE, NY, USA (2002)

32. Tewfik, A., Mansour, M.: Secure watermark detection with non-parametric decision boundaries. In: Proc. of Int. Conf. on Acoustics, Speech and Signal Processing 2002 (ICASSP 2002), pp. 2089–2092. IEEE, Los Alamitos (2002)
33. Kalker, T., Haitsma, J., Oosteveen, J.: Issues with digital watermarking and perceptual hashing (2001)
34. Charikar, M.: Similarity estimation techniques from rounding algorithms. In: Proceedings of STOC 2002, pp. 380–388. ACM, New York (2002)
35. Kulyukin, V.A., Bookstein, A.: Integrated Object Recognition with Extended Hamming Distance (2000)
36. Cormen, T.H., Leiserson, C.E., Rivest, R.L., Stein, C.: Introduction to Algorithms, 2nd edn. MIT Press and McGraw Hill (2001)
37. Mittelholzer, T.: An information-theoretic approach to steganography and watermarking. In: Pfitzmann, A. (ed.) IH 1999. LNCS, vol. 1768, pp. 1–17. Springer, Heidelberg (2000)
38. Fabris, F.: Teoria dell'informazione, codici, cifrari. Boringhieri (2001)
39. Cover, T., Thomas, J.: Elements of Information Theory. John Wiley and Sons, New York (1991)
40. Maurer, U.M.: Authentication Theory and Hypothesis Testing. IEEE Transactions on Information Theory 46(4), 1350–1356 (2000)
41. Cachin, C.: An Information-Theoretic Model for Steganography. Information and Computation 192, 41–56 (2004)
42. Chandramouli, R., Subbalakshmi, K.P.: Current Trends in Steganalysis: A Critical Survey (2005)

Quantization-Based Methods: Additive Attacks Performance Analysis

J.E. Vila-Forcén[1,*], S. Voloshynovskiy[1,**], O. Koval[1],
F. Pérez-González[2], and T. Pun[1]

[1] Computer Vision and Multimedia Laboratory, University of Geneva, 24 Rue
Général-Dufour, 1204 Geneva, Switzerland
svolos@cui.unige.ch
[2] Departamento de Teoría de la Señal y Comunicaciones, ETSI Telecom., Universidad
de Vigo, 36200 Vigo

Abstract. The main goal of this study consists in the development of the worst case additive attack (WCAA) for $|\mathcal{M}|$-ary quantization-based data-hiding methods using as design criteria the error probability and the maximum achievable rate of reliable communications. Our analysis focuses on the practical scheme known as distortion-compensated dither modulation (DC-DM). From the mathematical point of view, the problem of the worst case attack (WCA) design using probability of error as a cost function is formulated as the maximization of the average probability of error subject to the introduced distortion for a given decoding rule. When mutual information is selected as a cost function, a solution of the minimization problem should provide such an attacking noise probability density function (pdf) that will maximally decrease the rate of reliable communications for an arbitrary decoder structure. The obtained results demonstrate that, within the class of additive attacks, the developed attack leads to a stronger performance decrease for the considered class of embedding techniques than the additive white Gaussian or uniform noise attacks.

1 Introduction

Data-hiding techniques aim at reliably communicating the largest possible amount of information under given distortion constraints. Their resistance against different attacks determine the possible application scenarios. The knowledge of the WCA allows to create a fair benchmark for data-hiding techniques and makes it possible to provide reliable communications with the use of appropriate error correction codes.

In general, digital data-hiding can be considered as a game between the data-hider and the attacker. This three-party two-players game was already investigated by Moulin and O'Sullivan [11] where two setups are analyzed. In the first one, the host is assumed to be available at both encoder and decoder prior to

---

* He is on leave to Universidad Carlos III de Madrid, Av. de la Universidad 30, 28911 Leganes, Madrid, Spain.
** The corresponding author.

Y.Q. Shi (Ed.): Transactions on DHMS III, LNCS 4920, pp. 70–90, 2008.
© Springer-Verlag Berlin Heidelberg 2008

the transmission, the so-called *private game*. In the second one, the host is only available at the encoder as in Fig. 1, i.e., the *public game*. The performance is analyzed with respect to the maximum achievable rate when the decoder is aware of the attacking channel and therefore maximum likelihood (ML) decoding is applied.

The knowledge of the attacking channel at the decoder is not a realistic assumption for most practical applications. Such a situation was analyzed by Somekh-Baruch and Merhav, who considered the data-hiding problem in terms of maximum achievable rates and error exponents. They assumed that the host data is available either at both encoder and decoder [15] or only at the encoder [16] and supposed that neither the encoder nor the decoder are aware of the attacker's strategy. In their consideration, the class of potentially applied attacks is significantly broader than in the previous study case [11] and includes any conditional pdf that satisfies a certain energy constraint.

Quantization-based data-hiding methods have attracted attention in the watermarking community. They are a practical implementation of a binning technique for channels whose state is non-causally available at the encoder considered by Gel'fand and Pinsker [7]. Recently it has been also demonstrated [12] that quantization-based data-hiding performance coincides with the spread spectrum (SS) data-hiding at the low-watermark-to-noise ratio (WNR) by taking into account the host statistics and by abandoning the assumption of an infinite image to watermark ratio.

The quantization-based methods have been widely tested against a fixed channel and assuming that the channel transition pdf is available at the decoder. A minimum Euclidean distance (MD) decoder is implemented as an equivalent of the ML decoder under the assumption of a pdf created by the symmetric extension of a monotonically non-increasing function [1].

It is a common practice in the data-hiding community to measure the performance in terms of the error rate for a given decoding rule as well as the maximum achievable rate of reliable communications. In this paper we will analyze the WCAA using both criteria.

In this paper we restrict the encoding to the quantization-based one and the channel to the class of additive attacks only. We assume that the attacker might be informed of the encoding strategy and also of the decoding one for the error exponent analysis, while both encoder and decoder are uninformed of the channel. Furthermore, the encoder is aware of the host data but not of the attacking strategy.

It is important to note that the optimality of the attack critically relies on the input alphabet even under power-limited attacks. McKellips and Verdu showed that the additive white Gaussian noise (AWGN) is not the WCAA for discrete input alphabets such as pulse amplitude modulation [10]. Similar conclusion for data-hiding was obtained by Pérez-González et al. [14], who demonstrated that the uniform noise attack performs worse than the AWGN attack for some WNRs. In [13], Pérez-González demonstrated that the AWGN cannot indeed be the WCAA because of its infinite support. Vila-Forcén et al. [18] and Goteti and Moulin [8] solved independently the min-max problem for the DC-DM [2] in terms of probability of error for the fixed decoder, binary signaling, the subclass of additive attacks in data-hiding and detection-formulation, respectively.

Simultaneously, Vila-Forcén et al. [19] and Tzoschoppe et al. [17] derived the WCAA for DC-DM using the mutual information as objective function for additive attacks.

This paper aims at establishing the information-theoretic limits of $|\mathcal{M}|$-ary quantization-based data-hiding techniques and developing a benchmark that can be used for the a comparison of different quantization-based methods.

The selection of the distortion compensation parameter α' (see Section 2.2) fixes the encoder structure for the quantization-based methods. Although the optimal α' can easily be determined when the power of the noise is available at the encoder prior to the transmission [5], this is not always feasible for various practical scenarios. Nevertheless, the availability of the attacking power and of the attacking pdf is a very common assumption in most data-hiding schemes. We will demonstrate that for a specific decoder (MD decoder) it is possible to calculate the optimal α' independently of the attack variance and pdf for the block error probability as a cost function.

The paper is organized as follows. Problem formulation is given in Section 2. The investigation of the WCAA for a fixed quantization-based data-hiding scenario is performed in Section 3, where the cost function is the probability of error. The information-theoretic analysis of Section 4 derives the information bounds where the cost function is the mutual information between the input message and the channel output.

Notations: We use capital letters to denote scalar random variables X, bold capital letters to denote vector random variables $\mathbf{X}$ and corresponding small letters x and $\mathbf{x}$ to denote the realizations of scalar and vector random variables, respectively. An information message and a set of messages with cardinality $|\mathcal{M}|$ is designated as $m \in \mathcal{M}, \mathcal{M} = \{1, 2, \ldots, |\mathcal{M}|\}$, respectively. A host signal distributed according to the pdf $f_{\mathbf{X}}(\mathbf{x})$ is denoted by $\mathbf{X} \sim f_{\mathbf{X}}(\mathbf{x})$; $\mathbf{Z} \sim f_{\mathbf{Z}}(\mathbf{z})$, $\mathbf{W} \sim f_{\mathbf{W}}(\mathbf{w})$ and $\mathbf{V} \sim f_{\mathbf{V}}(\mathbf{v})$ represents the attack, the watermark and the received signal, respectively. The step of quantization is equal to Δ and the distortion-compensation factor is denoted as α'. The variance of the watermark is σ_W^2 and the variance of the attack is σ_Z^2. The WNR is given by WNR $= 10 \log_{10} \xi$, where $\xi = \frac{\sigma_W^2}{\sigma_Z^2}$. The set of natural numbers is denoted as $\mathbb{N}$ and $\mathbb{I}_N$ denotes the $N \times N$ identity matrix.

2   Digital Data-Hiding: Binning Approach

2.1   Gel'fand-Pinsker Formulation of the Data-Hiding Problem

The Gel'fand-Pinsker problem [7] has been recently revealed as the appropriate theoretical framework of data-hiding communications with side information. The Gel'fand-Pinsker data-hiding setup is presented in Fig. 1. In order to communicate a message $m \in \mathcal{M}, \mathcal{M} = \{1, 2, \ldots, |\mathcal{M}|\}$, the encoder performs a mapping

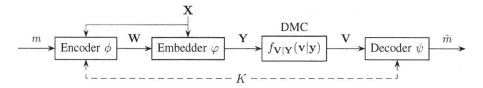

Fig. 1. Gel'fand-Pinsker data-hiding setup

$\phi : \mathcal{M} \times \mathcal{X}^N \times \mathcal{K} \to \mathcal{W}^N$ based on a non-causally available host realization $\mathbf{x} \in \mathcal{X}^N$ and the key $k \in \mathcal{K}, \mathcal{K} = \{1, 2, \ldots, |\mathcal{K}|\}$. The stego data $\mathbf{Y}$ is obtained using the embedding mapping: $\varphi : \mathcal{W}^N \times \mathcal{X}^N \to \mathcal{Y}^N$. The decoder estimates the transmitted message from the channel output as $\psi : \mathcal{V}^N \times \mathcal{K} \to \mathcal{M}$. According to this scheme, a key is available at both encoder and decoder. Nevertheless, key management is outside of the scope of this paper and we will not consider it further.

Two constraints apply to the Gel'fand-Pinsker framework in the data-hiding scenario: the embedding and the channel constraints [11]. Let $d(\cdot, \cdot)$ be a non-negative function and σ_W^2, σ_Z^2 be two positive numbers, the embedder is said to satisfy the embedding constraint if:

$$\sum_{\mathbf{x} \in \mathcal{X}^N} \sum_{\mathbf{y} \in \mathcal{Y}^N} d(\mathbf{x}, \mathbf{y}) f_{\mathbf{X},\mathbf{Y}}(\mathbf{x}, \mathbf{y}) \leq \sigma_W^2, \tag{1}$$

where $d(\mathbf{x}, \mathbf{y}) = \frac{1}{N} \sum_{i=1}^{N} d(x_i, y_i)$.

Analogously, the channel is said to satisfy the channel constraint if:

$$\sum_{\mathbf{y} \in \mathcal{Y}^N} \sum_{\mathbf{v} \in \mathcal{V}^N} d(\mathbf{y}, \mathbf{v}) f_{\mathbf{Y},\mathbf{V}}(\mathbf{y}, \mathbf{v}) \leq \sigma_Z^2. \tag{2}$$

Costa setup: Costa considered the Gel'fand-Pinsker problem for the independent and identically distributed (i.i.d.) Gaussian case and mean squared error distance [3]. The embedder φ produces $\mathbf{Y} = \mathbf{W} + \mathbf{X}$, $\mathbf{X} \sim \mathcal{N}(\mathbf{0}, \sigma_X^2 \mathbb{I}_N)$. It is possible to write the channel output as: $\mathbf{V} = \mathbf{X} + \mathbf{W} + \mathbf{Z}$, where $\mathbf{Z} \sim \mathcal{N}(\mathbf{0}, \sigma_Z^2 \mathbb{I}_N)$, and the estimate of the message $\hat{m}$ is obtained at the decoder given $\mathbf{V}$. In the Costa setup, α denotes an optimization parameter used for the codebook construction at the encoder selected to maximize the achievable rate when $\alpha_{\text{opt}} = \frac{\sigma_W^2}{\sigma_W^2 + \sigma_Z^2}$ assuming that the encoder knows in advance the noise variance. In this case, the proposed setup achieves host interference cancellation and:

$$R(\alpha_{\text{opt}}) = C^{\text{AWGN}} = \frac{1}{2} \log_2 \left(1 + \frac{\sigma_W^2}{\sigma_Z^2} \right) \tag{3}$$

that corresponds to the AWGN channel capacity without host interference.

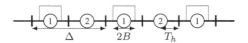

Fig. 2. DC-DM output pdf $f_{\text{DC-DM}}$ for the message $m = 1$ and binary signaling under high rate assumption

2.2 Quantization-Based Data-Hiding Techniques

Aiming at reducing the Costa codebook exponential complexity, a number of practical data-hiding algorithms exploit *structured codebooks* instead of random ones. The most famous discrete approximations to Costa problem are known as DC-DM [2] and scalar Costa scheme (SCS) [5]. The structured codebooks are designed using quantizers (or lattices [6]) which should achieve host interference cancellation.

Assuming that the channel transition pdf is given by some additive noise pdf, within the class of quantization-based methods, we focus our analysis on DC-DM and dither modulation (DM) [2].

For the DC-DM case, the stego data is obtained as follows:

$$\phi_{\text{DC-DM}}(m, x, \alpha') = y = x + \alpha'(Q_m(x) - x), \tag{4}$$

where $0 < \alpha' \le 1$ is the analogue of the Costa optimization parameter α. If $\alpha' = 1$, the DC-DM (4) simplifies to the DM ($\phi_{\text{DM}}(m, x) = y = Q_m(x)$). The embedding distortion for the DC-DM is $\sigma_W^2 = \alpha'^2 \frac{\Delta^2}{12}$. In this case, the pdf of the stego image is represented by a train of uniform pulses of width $2B = (1 - \alpha')\Delta$ centered at the quantizer reconstruction level as a result of the distortion compensation[1]. An example of such a pdf $f_{\text{DC-DM}}$ corresponding to the communications of the message $m = 1$ is given in Fig. 2 where $T_h = \frac{\Delta}{2|\mathcal{M}|}$ denotes the distance between two neighbor quantizer decision and reconstruction levels.

Using the MD decoding rule ($\hat{m}^{\text{MD}} = \text{argmin}_{m \in \mathcal{M}} ||v - Q_m(v)||^2$), the correct decoding region $\mathcal{R}_m$ and the complementary error region $\overline{\mathcal{R}}_m$ associated to a message m, are defined as it is depicted in Fig. 3 [14].

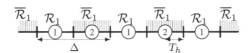

Fig. 3. DM and DC-DM correct decoding region $\mathcal{R}_1$ and error decoding region $\overline{\mathcal{R}}_1$ for the message $m = 1$ and binary signaling when the MD decoder is used

---

[1] The analysis is performed here in the framework of Eggers et al. [5] disregarding the host pdf impact. If host pdf is taken into account, we refer readers to [9, 12] for more details.

3   Error Probability as a Cost Function

When the average error probability is selected as a cost function, we formulate the problem of Fig. 1 as:

$$P_B^{*(N)} = \min_{\phi,\psi} \max_{f_{V|Y}(\cdot|\cdot)} P_B(\phi, \psi, f_{V|Y}(\cdot|\cdot)), \tag{5}$$

where $P_B(\phi, \psi, f_{V|Y}(\cdot|\cdot))$ is the average error probability for an encoder ϕ, decoder ψ and channel $f_{V|Y}(\cdot|\cdot)$, and $P_B^{*(N)}$ is the resulting error probability. The error probability depends on the particular encoder and decoder pair (ϕ, ψ) and the attacking channel $f_{\mathbf{V}|\mathbf{Y}}(\mathbf{v}|\mathbf{y})$, i.e., $P_B(\phi, \psi, f_{V|Y}(v|y)) = \Pr[\hat{m} \neq m | M = m]$. Here, we assume that the attacker knows both encoder and decoder strategies and selects its attacking strategy accordingly. Both encoder and decoder select their strategy without knowing the attack in advance. Although this is a very conservative setup, it is also important for various practical scenarios.

The more advantageous setup for the data-hider is based on the assumption that the decoder selects its strategy knowing the attacker choice:

$$\min_{\phi} \max_{f_{V|Y}(\cdot|\cdot)} \min_{\psi} P_B(\phi, \psi, f_{V|Y}(\cdot|\cdot)). \tag{6}$$

Here, the attacker knows only the encoding function, which is fixed prior to the attack, and the decoder is assumed to be aware of the attack pdf.

In the general case, Somekh-Baruch and Merhav [15] have shown the following inequalities for the above scenarios:

$$\min_{\phi,\psi} \max_{f_{V|Y}(\cdot|\cdot)} P_B(\phi, \psi, f_{V|Y}(\cdot|\cdot)) \geq \min_{\phi} \max_{f_{V|Y}(\cdot|\cdot)} \min_{\psi} P_B(\phi, \psi, f_{V|Y}(\cdot|\cdot)) \tag{7}$$

$$= \min_{\phi} \max_{f_{V|Y}(\cdot|\cdot)} P_B(\phi, \psi^{\mathrm{ML}}, f_{V|Y}(\cdot|\cdot)), \tag{8}$$

where the equality (8) is a consequence of the fact that the decoder is aware of the attacking pdf and therefore the minimization at the decoder results in the optimal ML decoding strategy ψ^{ML}.

In the analysis of the WCAA using the error probability as a cost function, we will further assume that the MD decoder is applied.

In the class of additive attacks, the attacking channel transition pdf is only determined by the pdf of the additive noise $f_Z(z)$. Finally, in this analysis we assume independence of the error probability on the quantization bin where the received signal v lies (because the error region $\overline{\mathcal{R}}_m$ (Fig. 3) has periodical structure and the host pdf $f_X(x)$ is assumed to be asymptotically constant within each quantization bin).

Applying (7) to the quantization-based data-hiding (Section 2.2) and assuming an additive attacking scenario, the MD decoding rule and high-rate, one has:

$$\min_{\alpha'} \max_{f_Z(\cdot)} P_B(\alpha', \psi^{\mathrm{MD}}, f_Z(\cdot)) \geq \min_{\alpha'} P_B(\phi, \psi^{\mathrm{MD}}, \tilde{f}_Z(\cdot)), \tag{9}$$

where the equality holds if, and only if, the fixed attack pdf $\tilde{f}_Z(z)$ coincides with the WCAA. Here, the encoder optimization is reduced to the selection of an optimal parameter α' since Δ is fixed by the embedding constraint, and the channel is reduced to the selection of the worst additive noise pdf.

The problem (9) implies that the attacker might know both encoding and decoding strategy. Here, we target finding the WCAA pdf and the optimum fixed encoding strategy independently of the particular attacking case which guarantees reliable communications and provides an upper bound on the error probability.

Considering the previously discussed quantization-based techniques and the MD decoder, and assuming that the message m is communicated, the probability of correct decoding P_B^c is determined as [14]:

$$
\begin{aligned}
P_B^c &= \Pr[||V - Q_m(V)||^2 < ||V - Q_{m'}(V)||^2 : \forall \, m' \in \mathcal{M}, m' \neq m] \\
&= \Pr[V \in \mathcal{R}_m | M = m]. \tag{10}
\end{aligned}
$$

The error probability can be obtained as $P_B = 1 - P_B^c$. We can represent the error probability as the integral of the equivalent noise pdf $f_{Z_{eq}|M} = f_Z * f_{\text{DC-DM}}$ over the error region $\overline{\mathcal{R}}_m$:

$$
P_B = \frac{1}{|\mathcal{M}|} \int_{\overline{\mathcal{R}}_m} f_{Z_{eq}|M}(z_{eq}|M = m) dz_{eq}. \tag{11}
$$

For the $|\mathcal{M}|$-ary case, it is possible to write the probability of error as a sum of integrals as:

$$
P_B = 2 \frac{1}{|\mathcal{M}|} \sum_{k=0}^{\infty} \int_{k\Delta + \Delta/2|\mathcal{M}|}^{(k+1)\Delta - \Delta/2|\mathcal{M}|} f_{Z_{eq}|M}(z_{eq}|M = m) dz_{eq}. \tag{12}
$$

In the case of DC-DM the pdf is given by the convolution of the attacking pdf with the self-noise pdf (periodic uniform pdf, Fig. 2) [14].

The following subsections are dedicated to the analysis of the error probability (12) for the WCAA as well as for the AWGN and uniform noise attacks.

3.1   The WCAA

The problem of the WCAA for digital communications based on binary pulse amplitude modulation (PAM) was considered in [10] using the error probability under attack power constraint. In this paper, the problem of the WCAA is addressed for the quantization-based data-hiding methods. The problem can be formulated as the left-hand part of (9), where the encoder is optimized over all α' such that $0 < \alpha' \leq 1$, and the attacker selects the attack pdf $f_Z(\cdot)$ maximizing the error probability P_B. Since the encoder must be fixed in advance in the practical setups, we will first solve the above min-max problem as an internal maximization problem for a given encoder/decoder pair:

$$
\max_{f_Z(\cdot)} P_B(\alpha', \psi^{\text{MD}}, f_Z(\cdot)) = \max_{f_Z(\cdot)} \int_{\overline{\mathcal{R}}_m} f_{Z_{eq}}(z_{eq}|M = m) dz_{eq}, \tag{13}
$$

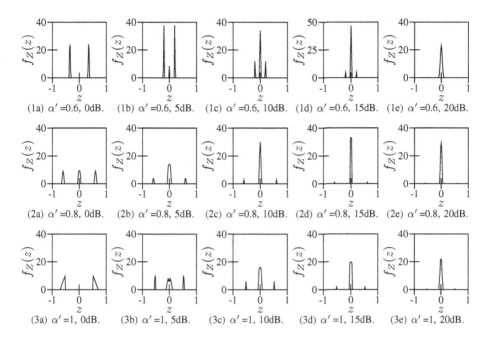

Fig. 4. WCAA optimization resulting pdfs for different α' and WNR, binary signaling

subject to the constraints:

$$\int_{-\infty}^{\infty} f_Z(z)dz = 1, \qquad \int_{-\infty}^{\infty} z^2 f_Z(z)dz \leq \sigma_Z^2, \tag{14}$$

where the first constraint follows from the pdf definition and σ_Z^2 constrains the attack power.

We will derive the WCAA based on (13) for a fixed α' and use it for the solution of (9) accordingly. The distortion compensation parameter α' leading to the minimum error probability will be the solution to (9).

Unfortunately, no close analytical solution has been found. The resulting attacking pdfs obtained using numerical optimization are presented in Figs. 4 and 5 for different WNRs and α' values assuming $\Delta = 2$.

The obtained pdfs are non-monotonic functions. Thus, the MD decoder is not equivalent to the ML decoder. The obtained error probability is depicted in Fig. 7, where its maximum is equal to 1 since we are assuming a fixed decoder (MD decoder). In a different decoding scenario when it is possible to invert the bit values, the maximum error probability will be equal to 0.5.

The broad variability of the obtained pdfs is not very convenient and tractable for various practical applications. Unfortunately, there is no close form approximation to the whole range of considered WNRs. Therefore, motivated by simplicity and benchmarking purposes, we have chosen an approximation based on a so-called $3 - \delta$ attack whose pdf is presented in Fig. 6, where T denotes the

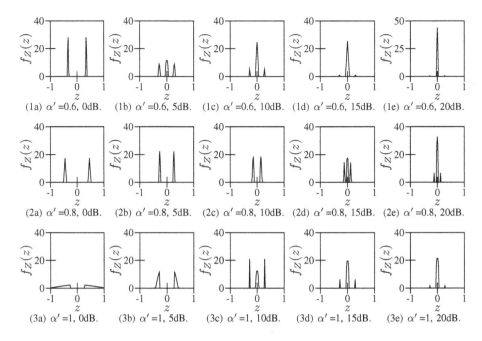

Fig. 5. WCAA optimization resulting pdfs for different α' and WNR, quaternary signaling

position of the lateral deltas and A their height. The $3 - \delta$ attack is a good approximation to the pdfs obtained in the medium and high-WNRs and provides a simple and powerful attacking strategy, which approximates the WCAA and might be used for testing different data-hiding algorithms. In order to demonstrate how accurate this approximation is, one needs to compare the average error probability caused by this attack versus the numerically obtained results.

For this purpose, the optimization of the $3 - \delta$ attack parameters has been performed for the DC-DM considering the DM as a particular case for $\alpha' = 1$. When $T - B < T_h = \frac{\Delta}{2|\mathcal{M}|}$, the error probability is equal to the integral of the equivalent noise pdf $f_{Z_{eq}|M}(z_{eq}|M = m)$ over the error region $\overline{\mathcal{R}}_m$ that can be found analitically:

$$P_B = \frac{A}{B}(T + B - T_h),\tag{15}$$

Fig. 6. $3 - \delta$ attack, $0 \le A \le 0.5$

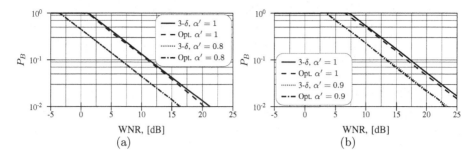

Fig. 7. Error probability comparison between the numerical optimization results and the $3 - \delta$ attack case: (a) binary signaling and (b) quaternary signaling

where $2B = (1 - \alpha')\Delta$ and $A = \frac{\sigma_Z^2}{2T^2}$. It is maximized for the following selection of $T = T_{opt_1}$:

$$T_{opt_1} = \frac{\Delta(1 - |\mathcal{M}|(1 - \alpha'))}{|\mathcal{M}|}. \tag{16}$$

The value of T_{opt_1} should be always positive, implying that $\alpha' > \frac{|\mathcal{M}|-1}{|\mathcal{M}|}$. It can be demonstrated that $T_{opt_1} \to 0$ as $\alpha' \to \frac{|\mathcal{M}|-1}{|\mathcal{M}|}$. For a given attack variance $\sigma_Z^2 = 2T^2 A > 0$ and $T_{opt_1} \to 0$, one has $A \to 0.5$ (its maximum value to satisfy the technical requirement to pdf in Fig. 6). Simplifying (15) for $\alpha' \to \frac{|\mathcal{M}|-1}{|\mathcal{M}|}$ implies that $P_B \to 1$. Thus, $A = 0.5$ and $P_B = 1$ for $\alpha' \le \frac{|\mathcal{M}|-1}{|\mathcal{M}|}$.

If $\alpha' > \frac{|\mathcal{M}|-1}{|\mathcal{M}|}$ and $T = T_{opt_1}$, the error probability is given by:

$$P_B = \frac{\sigma_Z^2 |\mathcal{M}| \alpha'^2}{24 \cdot \sigma_W^2 (1 - \alpha')(1 - |\mathcal{M}|(1 - \alpha'))}. \tag{17}$$

This result is valid if $T_{opt_1} - B < T_h$, and this constraint implies that $\alpha' \le 1 - \frac{1}{3|\mathcal{M}|}$. For this case, the minimum of the error probability is achieved at:

$$\alpha'_{opt} = \frac{2(|\mathcal{M}| - 1)}{2|\mathcal{M}| - 1}. \tag{18}$$

In case the previous condition does not hold ($\alpha' > 1 - \frac{1}{3|\mathcal{M}|}$), the error probability is calculated as: $P_B = 2A$. The maximum is found for the minimum possible $T = T_{opt_2} = T_h + B$, and the error probability is:

$$P_B = \frac{\sigma_Z^2 |\mathcal{M}|^2 \alpha'^2}{3 \cdot \sigma_W^2 (1 + |\mathcal{M}|(1 - \alpha'))^2}. \tag{19}$$

The comparison presented in Fig. 7 demonstrates that the 3-δ attack produces asymptotically the same error probability as the numerical optimization results presented in Figs. 4 and 5.

The optimization results (Figs. 4 and 5) demonstrate that for very low-WNR the WCAA structure does not necessarily corresponds to the 3-δ attack. Nevertheless, the 3-δ attack is a good approximation to the WCAA despite of its simplicity as shown in Fig. 7.

3.2   AWGN Attack

This Section contains the error probability analysis of the $|\mathcal{M}|$-ary DM and DC-DM techniques under the AWGN attack.

DM analysis: In the DM case, the equivalent noise pdf is given by a train of Gaussian functions:

$$f_{Z_{eq}|M}(z_{eq}|M = m) = \frac{1}{\sqrt{2\pi\sigma_Z^2}} e^{-\frac{z_{eq}^2}{2\sigma_Z^2}}, \qquad (20)$$

where σ_Z^2 denotes the variance of the attack. The error probability can be therefore calculated using (12).

DC-DM analysis: In the DC-DM case the equivalent noise pdf is given by [14]:

$$f_{Z_{eq}|M}(z_{eq}|M = m) = \frac{1}{2B}\left(\mathcal{Q}\left(\frac{z_{eq} - B}{\sigma_Z}\right) - \mathcal{Q}\left(\frac{z_{eq} + B}{\sigma_Z}\right)\right),$$

where $\mathcal{Q}$ is the $\mathcal{Q}$-function $\left(\mathcal{Q}(x) = \frac{1}{\sqrt{2\pi}}\int_0^x e^{-t^2/2}dt\right)$ and B is the half-width of the self-noise pdf. The analytical expression for the error probability (11) does not exist, and it is evaluated numerically using (12).

3.3   Uniform Noise Attack

It was shown [14] that the uniform noise attack produces higher error probability than the AWGN attack for some particular WNR in the binary signaling case. This fact contradicts the common belief that the AWGN is the WCAA for all data-hiding methods since it has the highest differential entropy among all pdfs with bounded variance. We consider the uniform noise attack $Z \sim \mathcal{U}(-\eta, \eta)$ with variance $\sigma_Z^2 = \frac{\eta^2}{3}$.

DM analysis: The equivalent noise pdf is given by a train of uniform pulses. In the case when the power of the attack is not strong enough, i.e., all noise samples are within the quantization bin of the sent message, the error probability is zero. For stronger attacks the error probability is defined by the integral of the equivalent noise pdf (a uniform pdf) over the error region using (12). The analytical solution when $\eta < \frac{2|\mathcal{M}|+1}{|\mathcal{M}|}\frac{\Delta}{2}$ in the $|\mathcal{M}|$-ary case is:

$$P_B(\alpha' = 1, \psi^{MD}, f_Z^{Unif.}(\cdot)) = \begin{cases} 0, & \eta < \frac{\Delta}{2|\mathcal{M}|}; \\ 1 - \frac{\Delta}{2|\mathcal{M}|\eta}, & \frac{\Delta}{2|\mathcal{M}|} \leq \eta < \frac{2|\mathcal{M}|-1}{|\mathcal{M}|}\frac{\Delta}{2}; \\ \frac{\Delta}{\eta}\frac{|\mathcal{M}|-1}{|\mathcal{M}|}, & \frac{2|\mathcal{M}|-1}{|\mathcal{M}|}\frac{\Delta}{2} \leq \eta < \frac{2|\mathcal{M}|+1}{|\mathcal{M}|}\frac{\Delta}{2}. \end{cases} \qquad (21)$$

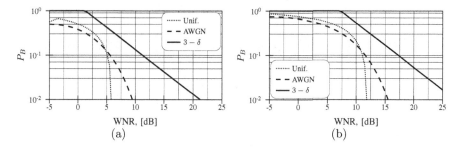

Fig. 8. Error probability analysis results for different attacking strategies: (a) DM performance and (b) DC-DM for $\alpha' = 0.8$ performance and binary signaling

In the third case, the error probability decreases while the WNR decreases as well. This effect is caused by the entrance of the noise into the nearest correct region and a smaller portion of the attack power is present in the error region. Because of this effect we have a non strictly decreasing probability of error as a function of the WNR. If $\eta > \frac{2|\mathcal{M}|+1}{|\mathcal{M}|}\frac{\Delta}{2}$, the error probability starts increasing again since the received pdf enters again the error region.

DC-DM Analysis: Under the uniform noise attack, the bit error probability is equal to the integral of the equivalent noise pdf $f_{Z_{eq}|M}(z_{eq}|M=m)$ (a train of trapezoidal functions) over the error region (12). The resulting analytical equation for $\eta + B < \Delta - T_h$ in the $|\mathcal{M}|$-ary case is:

$$P_B(\alpha', \psi^{MD}, f_Z^{Unif.}(\cdot)) = \begin{cases} 0, & T_h > \eta + B; \\ \frac{k_1}{8|\mathcal{M}|^2}, & |\eta - B| < T_h < \eta + B; \\ \min\{\frac{1}{2B}, \frac{1}{2\eta}\} \cdot k_2, & T_h < |\eta - B|, \end{cases} \quad (22)$$

where $k_1 = (2(\eta + B)|\mathcal{M}| - \Delta)(2m|\mathcal{M}|(\eta + B) + 4n|\mathcal{M}| + m\Delta)$, $k_2 = \left(\frac{(\eta+B)-|\eta-B|}{2} + ((\eta - B) - T_h)\right)$, $m = \frac{\min\{1/2B, 1/2\eta\}}{|\eta-B|-(\eta+B)}$ and $n = -m(\eta + B)$. If $\eta + B > \Delta - T_h$, the error probability decreases as in the DM case.

3.4 Error Probability Analysis Conclusions

The efficiency of the AWGN and the uniform noise attacks is compared with the 3-δ attack in Fig. 8, demonstrating that the gap between the AWGN attack and the $3 - \delta$ approximation of the WCAA can be larger than 5decibel (dB) in terms of the WNR.

The error probability as a function of the distortion compensation parameter for a given WNR demonstrates that the $3 - \delta$ attacking scheme is worse than either the uniform or Gaussian ones (Fig. 9). If the noise pdf is known, it is possible to select such an α' that minimizes the error probability for the given WNR in Fig. 9. For example, if WNR = 0dB and Gaussian noise is applied, the optimal distortion compensation factor is $\alpha' = 0.53$, resulting in $P_B = 0.23$.

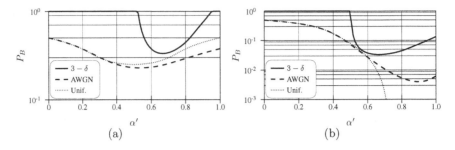

Fig. 9. Error probability comparison as a function of the distortion compensation parameter for the $3 - \delta$, Gaussian and uniform attacks and binary signaling: (a) WNR = 0dB and (b) WNR = 10dB

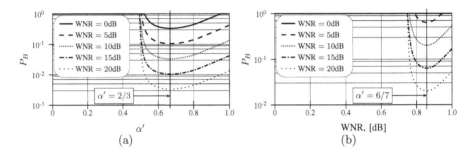

Fig. 10. Error probability analysis results as a function of the distortion compensation parameter α' for the $3 - \delta$ attack: (a) binary signaling and (b) quaternary signaling

Nevertheless, the encoder and the decoder are in general uninformed of the attacking strategy in advance and a mismatch in the attacking scheme may cause a bit error probability of 1, while for $\alpha' = 0.66$ the maximum bit error probability is $P_B = 0.33$.

According to the optimal compensation parameter given by (18), one can conclude that, independently of the operational WNR, $\alpha' = \alpha'_{opt}$ guarantees the lowest error probability of the analyzed data-hiding techniques under the $3 - \delta$ attack (Fig. 10). Having this bound on the error probability, it is possible to guarantee reliable communications using proper error correction codes. Therefore, one can select such a fixed distortion compensation parameter $\alpha' = \alpha'_{opt}$ at the uninformed encoder and the MD decoder, which guarantees a bounded error probability. Substituting (18) into (17), one obtains the upper bound on the error probability under the $3 - \delta$ approximation of the WCAA:

$$P_B(\alpha'_{opt}) = \frac{1}{6}|\mathcal{M}|(|\mathcal{M}| - 1)\xi^{-1}. \tag{23}$$

4   Mutual Information as a Cost Function

The analysis of the WCA with mutual information as a cost function provides the information-theoretic performance limit (in terms of achievable rate of reliable communications) that can be used for benchmarking of different practical robust data-hiding techniques.

Moulin and O'Sullivan [11] considered the maximum achievable rate in the Gel'fand-Pinsker setup (Section 2) as a max-min problem:

$$C = \max_{\phi} \min_{f_{V|Y}(\cdot|\cdot)} [I(U;V) - I(U;X)], \tag{24}$$

for a blockwise memoryless attack, the embedder distortion constraint σ_W^2 and the attacker distortion constraint σ_Z^2.

In the case of practical quantization-based methods the mutual information is measured between the communicated message M and the channel output V [13]: $I_{\phi,f_{V|Y}(\cdot|\cdot)}(M;V)$, where the subscript means that the mutual information depends on both encoder design and attack pdf.

It was shown in [13] that modulo operation does not reduce the mutual information between V and M if the host is assumed to be flat within the quantization bins. Consequently:

$$I_{\phi,f_{V|Y}(\cdot|\cdot)}(M;V) = I_{\phi,f_{V|Y}(\cdot|\cdot)}(M;V'), \tag{25}$$

where $V' = Q_\Delta(V) - V$, and the above problem can be reformulated as:

$$\max_{\phi} \min_{f_{V|Y}(\cdot|\cdot)} I_{\phi,f_{V|Y}(\cdot|\cdot)}(M;V'). \tag{26}$$

Rewriting the inequalities (7)–(8) for the mutual information as a cost function, we have:

$$\max_{\phi} \min_{f_{V|Y}(\cdot|\cdot)} I_{\phi,f_{V|Y}(\cdot|\cdot)}(M;V') \leq \max_{\phi} I_{\phi,\tilde{f}_{V|Y}(\cdot|\cdot)}(M;V'),$$

with equality if, and only if, the fixed attack $\tilde{f}_{V|Y}(\cdot|\cdot)$ coincides with the WCA. Thus, the decoder in Fig. 1 is not fixed and we assume that the channel attack pdf $f_{V|Y}(\cdot|\cdot)$ is available at the decoder (informed decoder) and, consequently, ML decoding is performed. Under previous assumptions of quantization-based embedding and additive attack, it is possible to rewrite (26) as:

$$\max_{\alpha'} \min_{f_Z(\cdot)} I_{\alpha',f_Z(\cdot)}(M;V'). \tag{27}$$

As for the error probability analysis case, we address the problem of the WCAA and the optimal encoding strategy for the WCAA. It is known [4] that the mutual information can be expressed in the general case as a Kullback-Leibler divergence (KLD):

$$I_{\alpha',f_Z(\cdot)}(M;V') = D(f_{MV'}(m,v')\|f_{V'}(v')p_M(m))$$
$$= \int f_{MV'}(m,v') \log_2 \frac{f_{V'|M}(v'|M=m)}{f_{V'}(v')} dv', \tag{28}$$

where $f_{M,V'}(m, v')$ is the joint pdf of the input message and the modulo of the channel output, $p_M(m)$ denotes the marginal probability mass function (pmf) of the input messages and $f_{V'}(v')$ the marginal pdf of the modulo of the channel output.

In fact, (28) can be written as the KLD between the received pdf when one of the symbols has been sent, and the average of the pdfs of all possible symbols. Assuming equiprobable symbols in the $|\mathcal{M}|$-ary signaling case, one obtains [13]:

$$I_{\alpha', f_Z(\cdot)}(M; V') = \frac{1}{|\mathcal{M}|} \sum_{m=1}^{|\mathcal{M}|} D\left(f_{V'|M}(v'|M = m)\|f_{V'}(v')\right)$$
$$= D\left(f_{V'|M}(v'|M = 1)\|f_{V'}(v')\right), \tag{29}$$

where:

$$D\left(f_{V'|M}(v'|M = m)\|f_{V'}(v')\right) = D\left(f_{V'|M}(v'|M = 1)\|f_{V'}(v')\right), \tag{30}$$

since $f_{V'|M}(v'|M = 1)$ and $f_{V'|M}(v'|M = m)$ are the same pdf shifted for all $m \in \mathcal{M}$ and $f_{V'}(v') = \frac{1}{|\mathcal{M}|} \sum_{m=1}^{|\mathcal{M}|} f_{V'|M}(v'|M = m)$.

The next subsections are dedicated to the analysis of the DM and the DC-DM under WCAA, AWGN attack and the uniform noise attack.

4.1   The WCAA

The problem of the WCAA using the mutual information as a cost function can be formulated using (27) and (29). Since the encoder must be fixed in advance as for the probability of error analysis case, we solve the max-min problem as a constrained minimization problem:

$$\min_{f_Z(\cdot)} I_{\alpha', f_Z(\cdot)}(M; V') = \min_{f_Z(\cdot)} D\left(f_{V'|M}(v'|M = 1)\|f_{V'}(v')\right), \tag{31}$$

where $0 < \alpha' \leq 1$. The constraints in (31) are the same as in the error probability oriented analysis case (14). Unfortunately, this problem has no closed form solution and it was solved numerically. The obtained results are presented for different α' values in Fig. 11.

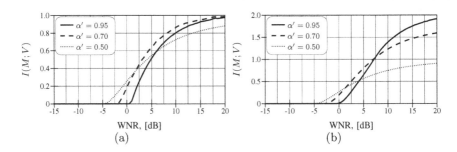

Fig. 11. Mutual information analysis results for the WCAA case: (a) binary signaling and (b) quaternary signaling

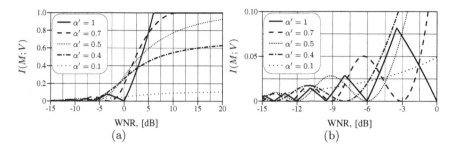

Fig. 12. Mutual information analysis results for the uniform noise attack case and binary signaling: (a) global performance analysis and (b) magnification of the low-WNR regime

4.2 AWGN Attack

When the DM and the DC-DM undergo the AWGN, no closed analytical solution to the mutual information minimization problem exists; the minimization was therefore performed using numerical computations.

4.3 Uniform Noise Attack

It was shown [14] that the uniform noise attack is stronger than the AWGN attack for some WNRs when the error probability is used as a cost function. One of the properties of the KLD measure states that it is equal to zero if, and only if, the two pdfs are equal. In case the uniform noise attack is applied, this condition holds for some particular values of WNR for the mutual information given by (29). It can be demonstrated that $I(M; V') = 0$ when $\xi = \frac{\alpha'^2}{k^2}, k \in \mathbb{N}$ for the $|\mathcal{M}|$-ary signaling. This particular behaviour allows the attacker to achieve zero rate of communication with smaller attacking power than was predicted by the data-hider. The mutual information of quantization-based data-hiding techniques for the uniform noise attacking case with binary and quaternary signaling is depicted in Fig. 12. It demonstrates that the efficiency of the attack

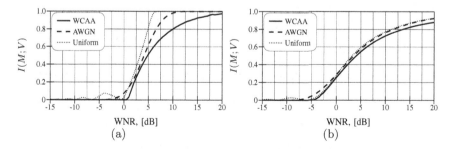

Fig. 13. Comparison of different attacks using mutual information as a cost function: (a) $\alpha' = 0.95$, binary signaling and (b) $\alpha' = 0.5$, binary signaling

strongly depends on the value of the distortion compensation parameter, and shows the oscillating behaviour at the low-WNR detailed in Fig. 12(b).

The uniform noise attack guarantees that it is not possible to communicate using the DC-DM at $\xi \leq \alpha'^2$, and therefore distortion compensation parameter α' has a strong influence on the performance at the low-WNR. As a consequence, $\xi = \alpha'^2$ represents the WNR corresponding to zero rate communication, if the attacking variance satisfies $\sigma_Z^2 \geq \frac{D_w}{\alpha'^2}$.

4.4   Mutual Information Analysis Conclusions

The results presented in Fig. 13 for various α' demonstrate that the developed attack produces the maximum loss in terms of mutual information for all WNRs in comparison with the AWGN or uniform noise attacks.

In the analysis of the WCAA using the error probability as a cost function, the optimal α' parameter was found. Unfortunately, it is not the case in the mutual information oriented analysis, and its value varies with the WNR. In Fig. 14 the optimum α' values as a function of the WNR are presented for several cardinalities of the input messages in comparison with the optimum SCS parameter [5]. It demonstrates that the SCS optimum distortion compensation parameter designed for the AWGN is also a good approximation for the WCAA case.

Recalling (27), we can conclude that it is not possible to find a unique optimum α' for the mutual information analysis case, contrarily to the error probability

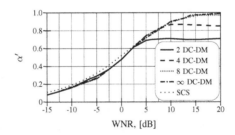

Fig. 14. Optimum distortion compensation parameter α' when the mutual information is selected as a cost function

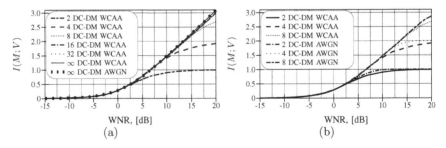

Fig. 15. Maximum achievable rate for different cardinalities of the input alphabet under the WCAA compared to the AWGN (a) for $|\mathcal{M}| \to \infty$ and (b) for $|\mathcal{M}| < \infty$

one when the decoder was fixed to the suboptimum MD decoder. Thus, the data-hider cannot blindly select a value of the distortion compensation blindly which guarantees reliable communications at any given WNR.

It is possible to observe a saturation of the optimum value of α' in Fig. 14 for small dimensionality and large WNR. Therefore, it is possible to select an optimum α' if the WNR range is known, located in the high-WNR regime and requirements of small dimensionality apply. For example, working in the high-WNR with WNR > 5dB and $|\mathcal{M}| = 2$, optimum α' can be chosen as $\alpha' = 0.71$.

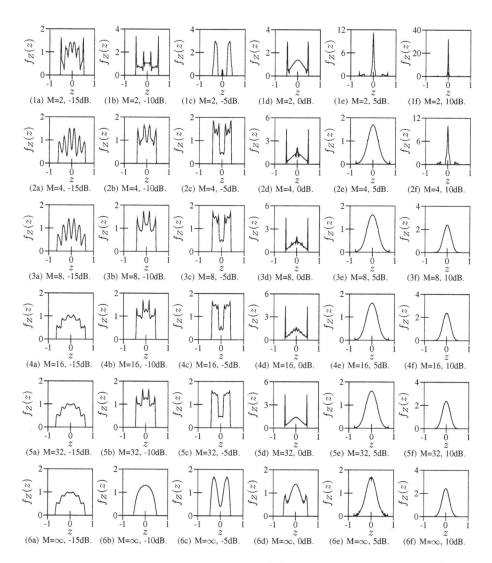

Fig. 16. Pdfs of the WCAA for different input distribution and WNRs

Using the optimum α' for each WNR, the resulting mutual information (31) is presented in Fig. 15(a) for different cardinalities of the input alphabet compared to the performance of the AWGN using the optimized $\alpha = \alpha_{opt}$ parameter [11]. The obtained performance demonstrates that the developed WCAA is worse than the AWGN whenever the optimum distortion compensation parameter is selected.

The pdfs of the WCAA for different cardinalities of the input alphabet and WNRs are depicted in Fig. 16. The results presented here have been obtained with a numerical optimization tolerance up to 10^{-12}.

Previous results [13] have already proven that the optimal WCAA pdf must be strictly inside the bin (and following the AWGN cannot be the WCAA). However, it is possible to achieve nearly optimal solutions with larger support of the pdf. The periodical repetition of the constellations yields a similar effective attack whilst using a larger power. In the presented experiments, the bin width was chosen as $\Delta = 2$.

The support of the presented WCAA pdfs does not vary significantly. The optimum distortion compensation parameter α' increments with the WNR and so the power of the embedded signal while the self-noise support decrements. Thus, the support of the attack remains nearly the same for all WNRs. Larger variations can be observed at the high-WNR and for high dimensionality, where the optimum α' variation is smaller.

It is possible to observe in Figs. 15(a) and 16 that the impact of the WCAA is very similar to a truncated Gaussian and that the difference in terms of the mutual information is negligible. Although the AWGN is not the WCAA, its performance is an accurate and practical approximation to the WCAA in the asymptotic case when $|\mathcal{M}| \to \infty$. For $|\mathcal{M}| < \infty$, the difference might be important for some WNRs and it is needed to consider the real WCAA as it is presented in Fig. 15(b).

5   Conclusions

In this paper we addressed the problem of the WCAA for the quantization-based data-hiding techniques from the probability of error and mutual information perspectives. The comparison between the analyzed cost functions demonstrated that in a rigid scenario with a fixed decoder, the attacker can decrease the rate of reliable communication more severely than by using either the AWGN or the uniform noise attacks. We showed that the AWGN attack is not the WCAA in general, and we obtained an accurate and practical analytical approximation to the WCAA, the so-called $3 - \delta$ attack, when the cost function is the probability of error for the fixed MD decoder. For the $3 - \delta$ attack, $\alpha' = \frac{2(|\mathcal{M}|-1)}{2|\mathcal{M}|-1}$ was found to be the optimal value for the MD decoder that allows to communicate with an upper bounded probability of error for a given WNR. This value could be fixed without prior knowledge of the attacking pdf.

The analysis results obtained by means of numerical optimization showed that there exists a worse attack than the AWGN when the mutual information was used as a cost function. Contrarily to the error probability analysis case, the optimal distortion compensation parameter (α') depends on the operational WNR for the mutual information analysis case. The particular behaviour of the mutual information under uniform noise attack was considered, achieving zero-rate communication for attacking variances σ_Z^2 such that $\sigma_Z^2 \geq \frac{D_w}{\alpha'^2}$. The presented results should serve as a basis for the development of fair benchmarks for various data-hiding technologies.

Acknowledgment

The authors acknowledge the valuable comments of the anonymous reviewers that helped to enhance the clarity and technical content of the paper. This paper was partially supported by SNF Professorship grant No PP002-68653/1, Interactive Multimodal Information Management (IM2) project and by the European Commission through the IST Programme under Contract IST-2002-507932 ECRYPT. The authors are thankful to the members of the Stochastic Image Processing group at University of Geneva and to Pedro Comesaña and Luis Pérez-Freire of the Signal Processing in Communications Group at University of Vigo for many helpful and interesting discussions. The information in this document reflects only the author's views, is provided as is and no guarantee or warranty is given that the information is fit for any particular purpose. The user thereof uses the information at its sole risk and liability.

References

1. Barni, M., Bartolini, F.: Watermarking Systems Engineering. Marcel Dekker, Inc., New York (2004)
2. Chen, B., Wornell, G.W.: Quantization index modulation: A class of provably good methods for digital watermarking and information embedding. IEEE Transactions on Information Theory 47(4), 1423–1443 (2001)
3. Costa, M.: Writing on dirty paper. IEEE Transactions on Information Theory 29(3), 439–441 (1983)
4. Cover, T., Thomas, J.: Elements of Information Theory. Wiley and Sons, New York (1991)
5. Eggers, J.J., Bäuml, R., Tzschoppe, R., Girod, B.: Scalar costa scheme for information embedding. IEEE Transactions on Signal Processing 51(4), 1003–1019 (2003)
6. Erez, U., Zamir, R.: Lattice decoding can achieve 0.5 log(1+snr) over the additive white gaussian noise channel using nested codes. In: IEEE International Symposium on Information Theory, Jun 2001, Washington DC, USA, p. 125 (2001)
7. Gel'fand, S.I., Pinsker, M.S.: Coding for channel with random parameters. Problems of Control and Information Theory 9(1), 19–31 (1980)
8. Goteti, A.K., Moulin, P.: QIM watermarking games. In: Proceedings of IEEE International Conference on Image Processing, vol. 2, pp. 717–720 (October 2004)
9. Koval, O., Voloshynovskiy, S., Pérez-González, F., Deguillaume, F., Pun, T.: Quantization-based watermarking performance improvement using host statistics: AWGN attack case. In: Proceedings of ACM Multimedia and Security Workshop, September 20-21, 2004, Magdeburg, Germany (2004)

10. McKellips, A., Verdu, S.: Worst case additive noise for binary-input channels and zero-threshold detection under constraints of power and divergence. IEEE Transactions on Information Theory 43(4), 1256–1264 (1997)
11. Moulin, P., O'Sullivan, J.: Information-theoretic analysis of information hiding. IEEE Transactions on Information Theory 49(3), 563–593 (2003)
12. Pérez-Freire, L., Pérez-González, F., Voloshynovskiy, S.: Revealing the true achievable rates of scalar costa scheme. In: IEEE International Workshop on Multimedia Signal Processing, September 29-October 1, 2004, Siena, Italy (2004)
13. Pérez-González, F.: The importance of aliasing in structured quantization modulation data hiding. In: International Workshop on Digital Watermarking, Seoul, Korea, pp. 1–17 (2003)
14. Pérez-González, F., Balado, F., Hernández, J.R.: Performance analysis of existing and new methods for data hiding with known-host information in additive channels. IEEE Transactions on Signal Processing, Special Issue on Signal Processing for Data Hiding in Digital Media and Secure Content Delivery 51(4), 960–980 (2003)
15. Somekh-Baruch, A., Merhav, N.: On the error exponent and capacity games of private watermarking systems. IEEE Transactions on Information Theory 49(3), 537–562 (2003)
16. Somekh-Baruch, A., Merhav, N.: On the capacity game of public watermarking systems. IEEE Transactions on Information Theory 49(3), 511–524 (2004)
17. Tzschoppe, R., Bäuml, R., Fischer, R., Kaup, A., Huber, J.: Additive Non-Gaussian Attacks on the Scalar Costa Scheme (SCS). In: Proceedings of IS&T/SPIE 17th Annual Symposium: Electronic Imaging 2005. Security, Steganography, and Watermarking of Multimedia Contents VII, vol. 5681, January 2005, San Jose, USA (2005)
18. Vila-Forcén, J.E., Voloshynovskiy, S., Koval, O., Pérez-González, F., Pun, T.: Worst case additive attack against quantization-based watermarking techniques. In: IEEE International Workshop on Multimedia Signal Processing, pp. 135–138, September 29-October 1, 2004, Siena, Italy (2004)
19. Vila-Forcén, J.E., Voloshynovskiy, S., Koval, O., Pérez-González, F., Pun, T.: Worst case additive attack against quantization-based data-hiding methods. In: Proceedings of IS&T/SPIE 17th Annual Symposium: Electronic Imaging 2005. Security, Steganography, and Watermarking of Multimedia Contents VII, January 16-20, 2005, San Jose, USA (2005)

Author Index

Bierbrauer, Jürgen   1

Fridrich, Jessica   1

Gerling, Ekaterina   23

Imai, Hideki   23

Jamzad, Mansour   33

Kermani, Zahra Zahedi   33
Korzhik, Valery   23
Koval, O.   70

Morales-Luna, Guillermo   23

Pérez-González, F.   70
Pun, T.   70

Shikata, Junji   23

Venturini, Ilaria   50
Vila-Forcén, J.E.   70
Voloshynovskiy, S.   70

Lecture Notes in Computer Science

Sublibrary 4: Security and Cryptology

For information about Vols. 1– 3903
please contact your bookseller or Springer

Vol. 5037: S.M. Bellovin, R. Gennaro, A. Keromytis, M. Yung (Eds.), Applied Cryptography and Network Security. XI, 508 pages. 2008.

Vol. 5023: S. Vaudenay (Ed.), Progress in Cryptology – AFRICACRYPT 2008. XI, 415 pages. 2008.

Vol. 5019: J.A. Onieva, D. Sauveron, S. Chaumette, D. Gollmann, K. Markantonakis (Eds.), Information Security Theory and Practices. XII, 151 pages. 2008.

Vol. 4991: L. Chen, Y. Mu, W. Susilo (Eds.), Information Security Practice and Experience. XIII, 420 pages. 2008.

Vol. 4986: M. Robshaw, O. Billet (Eds.), New Stream Cipher Designs. VIII, 295 pages. 2008.

Vol. 4965: N. Smart (Ed.), Advances in Cryptology – EUROCRYPT 2008. XIII, 564 pages. 2008.

Vol. 4964: T. Malkin (Ed.), Topics in Cryptology – CT-RSA 2008. XI, 437 pages. 2008.

Vol. 4948: R. Canetti (Ed.), Theory of Cryptography. XII, 645 pages. 2008.

Vol. 4939: R. Cramer (Ed.), Public Key Cryptography – PKC 2008. XIII, 397 pages. 2008.

Vol. 4920: Y.Q. Shi (Ed.), Transactions on Data Hiding and Multimedia Security III. IX, 91 pages. 2008.

Vol. 4896: A. Alkassar, M. Volkamer (Eds.), E-Voting and Identity. XII, 189 pages. 2007.

Vol. 4893: S.W. Golomb, G. Gong, T. Helleseth, H.-Y. Song (Eds.), Sequences, Subsequences, and Consequences. X, 219 pages. 2007.

Vol. 4890: F. Bonchi, E. Ferrari, B. Malin, Y. Saygin (Eds.), Privacy, Security, and Trust in KDD. IX, 173 pages. 2008.

Vol. 4887: S.D. Galbraith (Ed.), Cryptography and Coding. XI, 423 pages. 2007.

Vol. 4886: S. Dietrich, R. Dhamija (Eds.), Financial Cryptography and Data Security. XII, 390 pages. 2007.

Vol. 4876: C. Adams, A. Miri, M. Wiener (Eds.), Selected Areas in Cryptography. X, 409 pages. 2007.

Vol. 4867: S. Kim, M. Yung, H.-W. Lee (Eds.), Information Security Applications. XIII, 388 pages. 2008.

Vol. 4861: S. Qing, H. Imai, G. Wang (Eds.), Information and Communications Security. XIV, 508 pages. 2007.

Vol. 4859: K. Srinathan, C.P. Rangan, M. Yung (Eds.), Progress in Cryptology – INDOCRYPT 2007. XI, 426 pages. 2007.

Vol. 4856: F. Bao, S. Ling, T. Okamoto, H. Wang, C. Xing (Eds.), Cryptology and Network Security. XII, 283 pages. 2007.

Vol. 4833: K. Kurosawa (Ed.), Advances in Cryptology – ASIACRYPT 2007. XIV, 583 pages. 2007.

Vol. 4817: K.-H. Nam, G. Rhee (Eds.), Information Security and Cryptology - ICISC 2007. XIII, 367 pages. 2007.

Vol. 4812: P. McDaniel, S.K. Gupta (Eds.), Information Systems Security. XIII, 322 pages. 2007.

Vol. 4784: W. Susilo, J.K. Liu, Y. Mu (Eds.), Provable Security. X, 237 pages. 2007.

Vol. 4779: J.A. Garay, A.K. Lenstra, M. Mambo, R. Peralta (Eds.), Information Security. XIII, 437 pages. 2007.

Vol. 4776: N. Borisov, P. Golle (Eds.), Privacy Enhancing Technologies. X, 273 pages. 2007.

Vol. 4752: A. Miyaji, H. Kikuchi, K. Rannenberg (Eds.), Advances in Information and Computer Security. XIII, 460 pages. 2007.

Vol. 4734: J. Biskup, J. López (Eds.), Computer Security – ESORICS 2007. XIV, 628 pages. 2007.

Vol. 4727: P. Paillier, I. Verbauwhede (Eds.), Cryptographic Hardware and Embedded Systems - CHES 2007. XIV, 468 pages. 2007.

Vol. 4691: T. Dimitrakos, F. Martinelli, P.Y.A. Ryan, S. Schneider (Eds.), Formal Aspects in Security and Trust. VIII, 285 pages. 2007.

Vol. 4677: A. Aldini, R. Gorrieri (Eds.), Foundations of Security Analysis and Design IV. VII, 325 pages. 2007.

Vol. 4657: C. Lambrinoudakis, G. Pernul, A.M. Tjoa (Eds.), Trust, Privacy and Security in Digital Business. XIII, 291 pages. 2007.

Vol. 4637: C. Kruegel, R. Lippmann, A. Clark (Eds.), Recent Advances in Intrusion Detection. XII, 337 pages. 2007.

Vol. 4631: B. Christianson, B. Crispo, J.A. Malcolm, M. Roe (Eds.), Security Protocols. IX, 347 pages. 2007.

Vol. 4622: A. Menezes (Ed.), Advances in Cryptology - CRYPTO 2007. XIV, 631 pages. 2007.

Vol. 4593: A. Biryukov (Ed.), Fast Software Encryption. XI, 467 pages. 2007.

Vol. 4586: J. Pieprzyk, H. Ghodosi, E. Dawson (Eds.), Information Security and Privacy. XIV, 476 pages. 2007.

Vol. 4582: J. López, P. Samarati, J.L. Ferrer (Eds.), Public Key Infrastructure. XI, 375 pages. 2007.

Vol. 4579: B.M. Hämmerli, R. Sommer (Eds.), Detection of Intrusions and Malware, and Vulnerability Assessment. X, 251 pages. 2007.

Vol. 4575: T. Takagi, T. Okamoto, E. Okamoto, T. Okamoto (Eds.), Pairing-Based Cryptography – Pairing 2007. XI, 408 pages. 2007.

Vol. 4567: T. Furon, F. Cayre, G. Doërr, P. Bas (Eds.), Information Hiding. XI, 393 pages. 2008.

Vol. 4521: J. Katz, M. Yung (Eds.), Applied Cryptography and Network Security. XIII, 498 pages. 2007.

Vol. 4515: M. Naor (Ed.), Advances in Cryptology - EUROCRYPT 2007. XIII, 591 pages. 2007.

Vol. 4499: Y.Q. Shi (Ed.), Transactions on Data Hiding and Multimedia Security II. IX, 117 pages. 2007.

Vol. 4464: E. Dawson, D.S. Wong (Eds.), Information Security Practice and Experience. XIII, 361 pages. 2007.

Vol. 4462: D. Sauveron, K. Markantonakis, A. Bilas, J.-J. Quisquater (Eds.), Information Security Theory and Practices. XII, 255 pages. 2007.

Vol. 4450: T. Okamoto, X. Wang (Eds.), Public Key Cryptography – PKC 2007. XIII, 491 pages. 2007.

Vol. 4437: J.L. Camenisch, C.S. Collberg, N.F. Johnson, P. Sallee (Eds.), Information Hiding. VIII, 389 pages. 2007.

Vol. 4392: S.P. Vadhan (Ed.), Theory of Cryptography. XI, 595 pages. 2007.

Vol. 4377: M. Abe (Ed.), Topics in Cryptology – CT-RSA 2007. XI, 403 pages. 2006.

Vol. 4356: E. Biham, A.M. Youssef (Eds.), Selected Areas in Cryptography. XI, 395 pages. 2007.

Vol. 4341: P.Q. Nguyên (Ed.), Progress in Cryptology - VIETCRYPT 2006. XI, 385 pages. 2006.

Vol. 4332: A. Bagchi, V. Atluri (Eds.), Information Systems Security. XV, 382 pages. 2006.

Vol. 4329: R. Barua, T. Lange (Eds.), Progress in Cryptology - INDOCRYPT 2006. X, 454 pages. 2006.

Vol. 4318: H. Lipmaa, M. Yung, D. Lin (Eds.), Information Security and Cryptology. XI, 305 pages. 2006.

Vol. 4307: P. Ning, S. Qing, N. Li (Eds.), Information and Communications Security. XIV, 558 pages. 2006.

Vol. 4301: D. Pointcheval, Y. Mu, K. Chen (Eds.), Cryptology and Network Security. XIII, 381 pages. 2006.

Vol. 4300: Y.Q. Shi (Ed.), Transactions on Data Hiding and Multimedia Security I. IX, 139 pages. 2006.

Vol. 4298: J.K. Lee, O. Yi, M. Yung (Eds.), Information Security Applications. XIV, 406 pages. 2007.

Vol. 4296: M.S. Rhee, B. Lee (Eds.), Information Security and Cryptology – ICISC 2006. XIII, 358 pages. 2006.

Vol. 4284: X. Lai, K. Chen (Eds.), Advances in Cryptology – ASIACRYPT 2006. XIV, 468 pages. 2006.

Vol. 4283: Y.Q. Shi, B. Jeon (Eds.), Digital Watermarking. XII, 474 pages. 2006.

Vol. 4266: H. Yoshiura, K. Sakurai, K. Rannenberg, Y. Murayama, S.-i. Kawamura (Eds.), Advances in Information and Computer Security. XIII, 438 pages. 2006.

Vol. 4258: G. Danezis, P. Golle (Eds.), Privacy Enhancing Technologies. VIII, 431 pages. 2006.

Vol. 4249: L. Goubin, M. Matsui (Eds.), Cryptographic Hardware and Embedded Systems - CHES 2006. XII, 462 pages. 2006.

Vol. 4237: H. Leitold, E.P. Markatos (Eds.), Communications and Multimedia Security. XII, 253 pages. 2006.

Vol. 4236: L. Breveglieri, I. Koren, D. Naccache, J.-P. Seifert (Eds.), Fault Diagnosis and Tolerance in Cryptography. XIII, 253 pages. 2006.

Vol. 4219: D. Zamboni, C. Krügel (Eds.), Recent Advances in Intrusion Detection. XII, 331 pages. 2006.

Vol. 4189: D. Gollmann, J. Meier, A. Sabelfeld (Eds.), Computer Security – ESORICS 2006. XI, 548 pages. 2006.

Vol. 4176: S.K. Katsikas, J. López, M. Backes, S. Gritzalis, B. Preneel (Eds.), Information Security. XIV, 548 pages. 2006.

Vol. 4117: C. Dwork (Ed.), Advances in Cryptology - CRYPTO 2006. XIII, 621 pages. 2006.

Vol. 4116: R. De Prisco, M. Yung (Eds.), Security and Cryptography for Networks. XI, 366 pages. 2006.

Vol. 4107: G. Di Crescenzo, A. Rubin (Eds.), Financial Cryptography and Data Security. XI, 327 pages. 2006.

Vol. 4083: S. Fischer-Hübner, S. Furnell, C. Lambrinoudakis (Eds.), Trust and Privacy in Digital Business. XIII, 243 pages. 2006.

Vol. 4064: R. Büschkes, P. Laskov (Eds.), Detection of Intrusions and Malware & Vulnerability Assessment. X, 195 pages. 2006.

Vol. 4058: L.M. Batten, R. Safavi-Naini (Eds.), Information Security and Privacy. XII, 446 pages. 2006.

Vol. 4047: M. Robshaw (Ed.), Fast Software Encryption. XI, 434 pages. 2006.

Vol. 4043: A.S. Atzeni, A. Lioy (Eds.), Public Key Infrastructure. XI, 261 pages. 2006.

Vol. 4004: S. Vaudenay (Ed.), Advances in Cryptology - EUROCRYPT 2006. XIV, 613 pages. 2006.

Vol. 3995: G. Müller (Ed.), Emerging Trends in Information and Communication Security. XX, 524 pages. 2006.

Vol. 3989: J. Zhou, M. Yung, F. Bao (Eds.), Applied Cryptography and Network Security. XIV, 488 pages. 2006.

Vol. 3969: Ø. Ytrehus (Ed.), Coding and Cryptography. XI, 443 pages. 2006.

Vol. 3958: M. Yung, Y. Dodis, A. Kiayias, T. Malkin (Eds.), Public Key Cryptography - PKC 2006. XIV, 543 pages. 2006.

Vol. 3957: B. Christianson, B. Crispo, J.A. Malcolm, M. Roe (Eds.), Security Protocols. IX, 325 pages. 2006.

Vol. 3956: G. Barthe, B. Grégoire, M. Huisman, J.-L. Lanet (Eds.), Construction and Analysis of Safe, Secure, and Interoperable Smart Devices. IX, 175 pages. 2006.

Vol. 3935: D.H. Won, S. Kim (Eds.), Information Security and Cryptology - ICISC 2005. XIV, 458 pages. 2006.

Vol. 3934: J.A. Clark, R.F. Paige, F.A.C. Polack, P.J. Brooke (Eds.), Security in Pervasive Computing. X, 243 pages. 2006.

Vol. 3928: J. Domingo-Ferrer, J. Posegga, D. Schreckling (Eds.), Smart Card Research and Advanced Applications. XI, 359 pages. 2006.

Vol. 3919: R. Safavi-Naini, M. Yung (Eds.), Digital Rights Management. XI, 357 pages. 2006.